CREATIVE **OCCASIONS**

Sue Warden

WINDING
STAIR
PRESS

Cataloguing in Publication Data is available

Cover and interior design: Sari Naworynski
Interior photographs: Jerry Kostecki
Front cover photograph: José Crespo
Styling and propping: Kim McIlwaine, Marion Neven and Sue Warden
Cover photo: Make-up by Anne Rosenbloom
            Hair by Joe Giraldi, Many Faces, Oakville, ON

Although every effort has been made to ensure the accuracy of the material included in this book, neither the author nor the publisher is responsible or liable in the event of misinterpretation of instructions or product application.

This book is available at special discounts for bulk purchases by your group or organization for sales promotions, premiums, fundraising and seminars. For details, contact: Peter March, Stewart House Publishing Inc., Special Sales Department, 195 Allstate Parkway, Markham, Ontario, L3R 4T8. Toll Free 1-866-474-3478.

We acknowledge the financial support of the Government of Canada through the Book Publishing Industry Development Program for our publishing activities.

Stewart House Publishing Inc.
Toronto

Printed in Canada.

This book is dedicated to my sister Marion and my best friend Kim.
Without the devotion and talent of these two people,
this book would not have happened.

Contents

Chapter **One**
Gift-Wrapping Basics

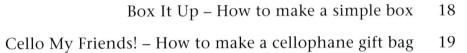

Chapter **Two**
Bow-Making

Chapter **Three**
Wedding Bells

Chapter **Four**
Baby Arrives

Chapter **Five**
Kids Create

Chapter **Six**
General Occasions

Chapter **Seven**
Cuisine Wrapped in Style

Chapter **Eight**
Make It A Memory

Chapter **Nine**
Christmas Creations

Chapter **Ten**
The Three R's
Reduce – Reuse – Recycle

Acknowledgments

This is the third book I have had the pleasure to write. With each book comes a little more experience in the publishing industry, and a greater appreciation for the dedication of the people it takes to make a book a success. Writing a book is more than having an idea. It is a team effort that takes determination, a good publisher, fabulous products and supportive companies. I consider myself extremely fortunate to have all of the above; wonderful companies who have graciously supported me with a never-ending flow of the latest product in the craft industry, a devoted team who believe in every project we embark upon, and a fabulous publishing house, full of great people who believe in what we do.

I know when you begin to make your own projects and create that special gift-wrap, you will appreciate the quality and endless choices that are available to you. Designers and companies devoted to the success of the craft industry make these choices possible. We are the lucky recipients of this great talent.

I see first-hand why crafting is so popular and why the craft industry is so successful. It is the devotion of these people, who are constantly developing new and unique ways to make our lives more decorative.

So thank you to the following companies and individuals whose continued success, drive and commitment to the industry help make my job easier and much more fun!

American Art Clay Co., Inc.

Armour Products

BagWorks Inc.

Currier Communications

DecoArt

Delta Technical Coatings, Inc.

Environmental Technology, Inc.

Essential Packaging

FPC Corporation - Surebonder

Fiskars Inc.

Hot Off The Press Inc.

Hunt Canada International

Loew-Cornell

The McCall Pattern Company

Mumby & Associates Limited

Offray Ribbon

Plaid Enterprises, Inc.

Provo Craft

Regal Greetings and Gifts

Panacea Products Corp.

Sanford

3M Canada Company

Walnut Hollow Woodcrafts

Westrim Crafts

Winward, A Lifestyle Company

To my sister Marion, who wears many hats at Sue Warden Visualmedia Inc.: Personal Assistant, Marketing and Publicity Director, Production Coordinator, Jill of all trades and master of all. Working with you is a childhood dream come true. Although we had to wait until the timing was right, it was well worth the wait. Thank you for all your hard work, devotion and love.

Designing, crafting and creating fabulous projects for our viewers and readers is our passion. This is probably the most important area of the company and requires devoted teamwork. To Kim, my best friend, Education and Design Manager, and Segment Producer extraordinaire, our 10-year friendship and working relationship has never been more important to me than it is today; a huge thanks for your constant enthusiasm and tireless effort in everything you do.

To all my friends and colleagues at Stewart House, Heather Bean, Sapna Jain, Marla Krisko, Joe March, Ralph Peter, Ken Proctor, Ken Thomson, designer Sari Naworynski, cover photographer José Crespo, Jerry Kostecki for fabulous interior photography that tells the story, and everyone involved in making this book a success. It is great to finally find a home. Thank you for making this project a complete pleasure, and for ensuring both past and present projects have met their potential and success.

I am where I am today because of the support and never-ending devotion of everyone I am involved with at Home & Garden and Life Television Networks. A gracious thanks to everyone in programming, Jim Erickson, Barb Williams, Vanessa Case; my Production Executive, Michael Quast; Marketing and Publicity, Walter Levitt, Jodi Cook, Sara Cooper, and of course a great editing department. Although I am unable to name everyone, my gratitude is sincere and I want to acknowledge my appreciation.

A huge thanks to my production team, in particular Andrea Darroch, a fabulous producer, friend and loyal supporter of everything we embark upon. Special thanks to those in production who have worked with us over the years: Bill Elliott, our Director, for his extreme professionalism; Gord Ross, our dynamic Director of Photography for his tireless efforts to make our shows a success; Anne Rosenbloom, who makes me look and feel great every day I'm in front of a camera; and everyone who we've worked with over the years. Your contribution to the show's success is unparalleled.

Last, but certainly not least, a huge thanks to you, our audience, viewers, readers and fellow crafts people. We are successful in bringing you great craft and home décor television programming, instruction books, and a comprehensive website, www.suewarden.com, because of your undying and enthusiastic response to all the information we pass along. Be happy, creative, and most of all, keep in touch. We love hearing from you.

Happy Wrapping

Sincerely, Sue

Introduction

I think we all love the act of giving. I know since I was very young, I much preferred to watch the faces of my family when I presented them with a gift than receive a gift myself (although I must admit, I love that too).

I have been creating and choosing gifts for many years, as most of us have. I really enjoy it when the recipient of my gift takes the time to appreciate the particular way in which I have wrapped or presented the gift. It may simply be the type of ribbon I have used, or perhaps I have incorporated some flowers into the bow, making it useful in the future. It doesn't have to be much – a little creativity goes a long way!

As of late, the trend in gift-wrapping has drifted somewhat from taking the time and care to wrap a gift, to purchasing a gift bag and quickly inserting the gift into the bag – convenient, yes, but not very creative.

I believe that one-of-a-kind gifts deserve one-of-a-kind gift-wrapping, and making the wrap itself either part of the gift, or at the very least useful, is inspiring.

Fabulous gift-wrapping not only makes us feel good about the gift we are presenting, it also inspires us to incorporate the same ideas used on the gift-wrap into other decorative projects. If you can stencil something onto a piece of gift-wrap, you have started the learning process and can take that knowledge and stencil your powder room, or a child's bedroom. Once you have tried your hand at embossing gift-wrap, the sky is the limit on where you can incorporate that same technique.

So, when you think of presenting that special someone, be it your partner, sister, brother, mother or father with a gift, take the time to think about how you have wrapped the gift. Does the wrapping reflect the time spent on choosing or creating the gift? If the answer to this question is "no" or "sometimes" or even "most of the time," this book is going to be inspiring and will give you tons of great ideas on how to make that special gift a "work of art."

Creative Occasions, which incorporates 50 project ideas, wonderful photography, useful tips, bow-making, and information pertaining to tools, is designed to not only help in the wrapping department, but introduce you to a possible whole new world. Learn how to make the wrapping a part of the gift, create reusable items to embellish, incorporate ideas and techniques into home décor projects, and much more.

I hope you find *Creative Occasions* useful, inspiring and fun. Use it as a workbook and expand your horizons with respect to projects, products and great ways to make others smile!

Enjoy,

Sue

Cut It – Adhere It – Paint It – Decorate It!
Suggested Supplies

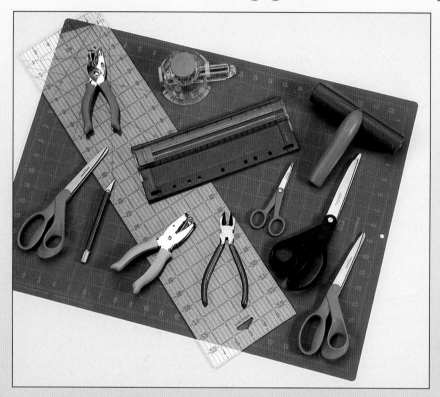

CUTTING AND
TRIMMING

ADHERING

PAINTING

FLORAL
DESIGNING

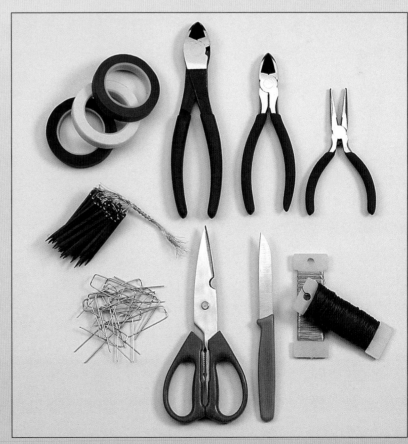

CHAPTER **ONE**

We've all been in the position, at one time or another, where we

have needed a gift wrapped quickly for an unexpected occasion.

Aside from the gift itself, ## Gift-Wrapping Basics

there's the question of how to wrap it quickly and creatively.

With some basic materials and a little ingenuity, you can have

your gift wrapped and ready for delivery before you know it.

From making your own gift box to wrapping those awkward

gifts, we'll guide you every step of the way.

HOW TO **MAKE A SIMPLE BOX**

Box It Up

Your gift will determine the type of box that needs to be made. Whatever you require, rest assured that the process is quick and easy. For this box, we used printed 3M Scotch Tape, which not only decorates the box, but also seals the edges at the same time.

Instructions:

① Begin by placing a large piece of cardboard on a flat surface.

② Measure and mark a square in the center of the cardboard of a size and shape that will accommodate the widest dimension of the gift.

③ Measure the height of the gift. Measure and mark the sides of the box in accordance with the height of the gift.

④ Cut the cardboard in a cruciform shape, following the markings.

⑤ Repeat this process to make the lid of the box, making the base size of the lid approximately 1/4" larger than the bottom of the box.

⑥ Fold the sides of the box up and seal each of the four sides using printed Scotch Tape edges.

⑦ Repeat this same process to create the box lid.

HOW TO
MAKE A CELLOPHANE GIFT BAG

Making your own cellophane bag is great fun. Cellophane wrap is easily purchased and relatively inexpensive, so the cost of this type of gift-wrapping is minimal. Because of the transparency of the cello, any colored or patterned tissue paper, fabric or material can be inserted into the bag, prior to the gift, to finish the look. Try using colored or printed cellophane for a different effect.

Cello My Friends!

Instructions:

① Begin by measuring the size of your gift.

② Cut a cardboard template as large as you want the bag to be, adding approximately 1" at the bottom.

③ Measure and cut a piece of the cellophane wrap twice the size of the cardboard template.

④ Lay the cellophane wrap on a flat work surface.

⑤ Place the template on the cellophane and wrap the cellophane around the template. Secure the joined cellophane edges with Scotch Tape.

⑥ Double fold the bottom edge of the cellophane and seal it with Scotch Tape. Remove the template.

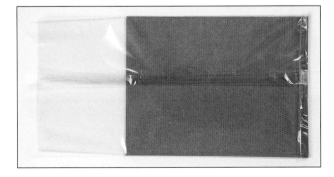

⑦ To finish the bag, insert a piece of tissue paper into the bag. Place the gift into the bag and tie with a piece of ribbon.

HOW TO
MAKE A PAPER GIFT BAG

This is a terrific option – making your own gift bag. These bags are especially beautiful when you incorporate handmade papers, découpage techniques, and gorgeous ribbons.

Instructions:

① To make your own gift bag, begin by selecting a book that is large enough to make a bag to fit your gift. Several books can be used, if necessary.

② Wrap the paper loosely around the book(s), allowing at least 1" for overlap, plus 2" for the base. Cut away the excess paper.

③ Lay the paper right-side down on a flat surface.

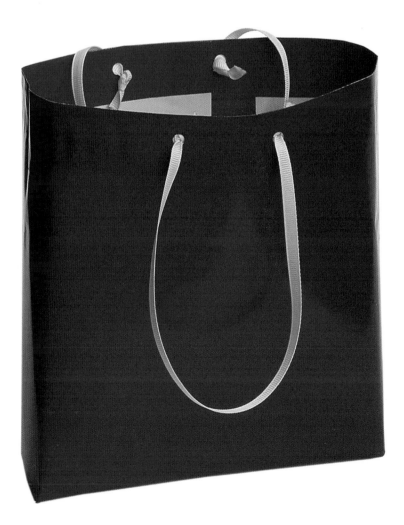

④ Fold one outside edge over by approximately 1/2". Fold one short edge down 1".

⑤ Lay the book(s) on the paper, allowing the paper to exceed the short end by approximately 2". Draw the long sides together over the book(s) and seal the long edges together using a glue stick.

⑥ To create the bottom of the bag, fold one side of the paper down flat against the book(s), creasing each side flap.

⑦ Fold each side flap in toward the center of the book(s), creasing it as you go. Adhere the side flaps using a glue stick.

⑧ Crease the bottom flap up toward the center point of the bottom of the bag. Fold the top of the flap over enough to have it meet the center point of the bottom of the bag. Adhere the flap to the bottom of the bag.

⑨ Remove the book(s) and stand the bag upright. Use a one-hole punch to evenly punch two holes 1/2" down from the top edge on one side of the bag. Repeat this process on the other side of the bag.

Paper Chase

⑩ Cut two lengths of cord, Wraphia or ribbon to make the handles. Insert one end of one length of ribbon through one hole from the outside in and tie a knot. Insert the other end of the ribbon through the second hole and knot the end to secure. Repeat with the second length of ribbon on the remaining side of the bag.

⑪ Decorate the bag to suit the occasion or to give a hint as to what lies inside!

HOW TO **MAKE A CONE**

Coney Island

Gift-wrapping using a cone shape is a unique way to present those awkward gifts that just defy being wrapped in anything! It's an especially pretty way of presenting a bouquet of flowers from your garden. You can also fill a cone shape with special chocolate or candy, or, even better, something from the kitchen. Regardless of the gift, the sentiment is always the same. Taking the time to wrap a gift in special ways says as much as the gift itself.

Instructions:

① Measure and cut a square of material such as corrugated, shiny or handmade paper. If you have a favorite wrapping paper, try crimping the paper before measuring and cutting.

② Lay the square of paper on a flat work surface, with one corner nearest you.

③ Measure and cut an arc from the left corner to the right corner, rounding the furthest corner of the square.

④ Roll the cone and overlap the edges until you have the required size. Adhere the edges, using a glue stick or Scotch Tape.

⑤ Decorate the cone, partly fill it with tissue paper or paper shred, and insert your gift.

⑥ Tie the cone with ribbon, Wraphia or twine, or adhere a piece of ribbon, if you want the cone to hang.

HOW TO **WRAP A ROUND GIFT**

As challenging as it may seem, wrapping a round gift is relatively easy. Using wrapping materials such as tissue, fabric or shrink-wrap makes the job fun and easy, while allowing for a lot of creativity. The trick is to ensure that you have allowed enough to accommodate the size of the object and for gathering at the top.

Round Robin

Instructions:

① Measure the dimensions of the gift and cut a piece of tissue paper to size. If you are using sheets of tissue and require more width, place two sheets criss-crossing one another.

② Place the gift in the center of the tissue paper and gather the paper around the gift. Make sure the tissue paper is drawn up all around the gift.

③ Tie a piece of ribbon around the gathered tissue paper as close to the gift as possible. If you are using fabric, use an elastic band around the gathered fabric and finish with ribbon.

④ If wrapping the gift with shrink-wrap, ensure that you have allowed enough wrap to cover the entire gift, adding approximately 2" extra for the top. When heat is applied to the wrap, it pulls in as it shrinks, so ensure that there are no open areas where the edges of the wrap meet. Finish the gift with decorative ribbons and tags.

HOW TO **WRAP A BOX**

Once you have decided how you wish to wrap your gift, make sure the box you choose is large enough to comfortably hold the gift. Create the box yourself or use a box you may have around the house. A box is simple, quick and readily available and can be wrapped using a myriad of papers. If you're stuck for paper, look up some of our ideas for creating simply beautiful wrapping paper, using freezer wrap or other materials you probably have on hand.

Box Car

Instructions:

① Begin by measuring the width and length of the box. Add 4" to each measurement.

② Measure and cut the wrapping paper in accordance with the above measurements.

③ Lay the paper right-side down on a flat surface.

④ Place the box, with the gift inside, upside down in the center of the wrong side of the paper.

⑤ Fold one long edge of the paper over by approximately 1". Lift both these edges to meet at the center of the bottom of the box. Place the folded edge on top of the

unfolded edge and adhere the edges together with Scotch Tape. Make sure the box is centered on the paper and the overlap fold line is centered on the box.

⑥ At one end of the "open" sides, fold one end of the paper down flat against the box, creasing each side flap. Fold each side flap in toward the center of the box. Crease the bottom flap in toward the center point. Fold the top of the flap over by approximately 1/4", or enough to allow it to meet at the center point of the box.

⑦ Fold the flap up and adhere it with a piece of Scotch Tape. Repeat this process on the remaining end of the box. Turn the box right-side up and wrap with ribbon.

HOW TO **WRAP A TUBE**

Tubular

Wrapping a tube is similar to wrapping a round gift. In the event the measurements of the gift are uneven, making a cardboard tube to encase your gift will make the wrapping smoother and easier.

Instructions:

① Measure your gift and cut a piece of cardboard to size. Wrap the cardboard around the gift and secure it with Scotch Tape or a glue stick.

② Place the wrapping paper of choice on a flat surface, right-side down.

③ Measure and cut the paper to fit the tube, allowing approximately 3" - 4" to extend on either end.

④ Place the tube close to one long side of the tissue paper. Roll the tube toward the opposite side. Secure with a piece of Scotch Tape or a glue stick.

⑤ Carefully gather the tissue paper on one end of the tube and tie with string or ribbon. Gather and tie the opposite end in the same manner.

HOW TO **WRAP A BOTTLE**

You've been invited to dinner at the last minute, and luckily you have a small cache of wine for such occasions. Now you face the challenge of wrapping it. Taking it unwrapped always seems a bit gauche, so here's a fast and easy way to solve the problem.

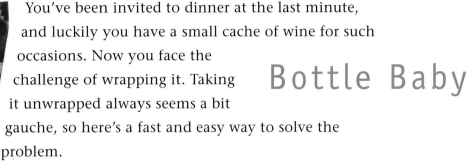

Any strong paper can be used, but the most efficient is corrugated paper. As this is something most of us don't usually have on hand, bristol board, brown mailing paper, construction paper or even-textured wallpaper work just as well. Crimping the paper will also provide the look of corrugated paper and add to the aesthetic look of the wrapping.

Instructions:

① Measure the dimensions of the bottle.

② Measure and cut a piece of paper to fit around the bottle, allowing 2" at the top and 1/2" overlap for the seam.

③ Place the bottle on the paper, with the base of the bottle even with the bottom edge of the paper.

④ Wrap the paper tightly around the bottle and secure the seam with Scotch Tape or glue strong enough to hold the paper in place.

⑤ Stand the bottle upright and decorate the top with ribbon, flowers, or other decorative elements.

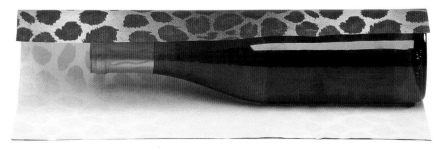

CHAPTER **TWO**

It doesn't seem to matter what time of year it is, bows are popular,

and everyone loves to learn how to make them. This chapter is a

complete lesson on making various types of

Bow-Making

bows for different projects, from giving that

tired old wreath a new look, to adding a little extra punch to

your decorated gift. Everyone is always amazed at how easy bow-

making really is.

HOW TO
MAKE A SIX-POINT BOW

Instructions:

① To make a six-point bow, measure and cut 9' of ribbon. Measure and cut an 8" piece of 24-gauge wire.

② Place one end of the ribbon, right-side out, in the palm of one hand and hold it securely with your thumb. Allow the length of ribbon to drape away from you.

③ Use your free hand to draw the ribbon around two fingers of the "holding" hand and secure the ribbon with your thumb to make one 2" loop.

④ Pinch the center bottom of the loop between your thumb and forefinger.

⑤ Hold the loop in one hand with the ribbon facing you. Continue to pinch the center of the loop between your thumb and forefinger.

⑥ Grasp the draping ribbon with the opposite hand and loop it under, to create a 3" loop. Pinch the ribbon between your thumb and forefinger. Continue this process of looping back and forth, each time pinching the ribbon into the middle section of the loop until there are three even loops on each side of the center loop.

⑦ Hold the ribbon firmly in the center to prevent the loops from springing apart. The remaining length of ribbon will be used to make the tails.

It's a Six-Pointer

⑧ Bring the end of the remaining length of ribbon up and pinch it under the center loop.

⑨ Insert an 8″ piece of 24-gauge floral wire through the center of the bow, and twist several times to secure the bow.

⑩ Cut the looped ribbon in half to create tails.

⑪ Trim the tail ends as desired. Adjust the loops on the bow.

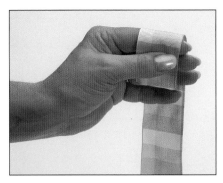

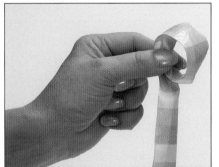

HOW TO **MAKE A FLORIST BOW**

Florist Flurry

Instructions:

① To make a florist bow, measure and cut 9′ of ribbon. Measure and cut an 8″ piece of 24-gauge floral wire.

② Measure 8″ from one end of the ribbon length and pinch between your thumb and forefinger in either hand.

③ Grasp the long end of the ribbon near the "holding" fingers and form a loop approximately 3″- 4″. Twist the ribbon under your thumb and forefinger.

④ Continue pinching the ribbon together. Twist the ribbon and bring it back up to form a second loop on the opposite side of the first.

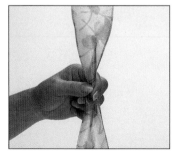

⑤ Continue twisting and looping until you have the desired even number of loops on either side of the center. Secure the loops by inserting an 8″ length of 24-gauge floral wire through the center and twisting the wire securely.

⑥ Trim both tails to an 8″ length.

⑦ Adjust the loops and finish the tails as desired.

HOW TO **MAKE A LOOPY BOW**

Loopy bows are best made with narrow ribbon, to allow for a soft look. Double-face satin ribbon works very well. Tucked inside a small floral arrangement or attached to the ribbon on a gift package, the loopy bow is very versatile.

Instructions:

① To make a loopy bow, measure and cut 9' of narrow satin ribbon. Measure and cut a small piece of 24-gauge floral wire.

② Hold (pinch) approximately 8" from one end of the ribbon. With your other hand, make one loop to the back.

③ Make a second loop to the front.

④ Continue looping the ribbon back and forth, until you have the desired number of loops. Do not twist the ribbon while making the loops.

⑤ When you have completed the desired number of loops, secure the bow with a small piece of 24-gauge floral wire.

Loop-de-Loop

HOW TO **MAKE A DOUBLE BOW**

Double the Fun

Double bows have a great impact, particularly when made of complementary or contrasting colors. To make a double bow, use wired ribbon. It gives the loops body and allows the bow to remain full.

Instructions:

① To make the bottom bow, measure and cut 9' of ribbon. Measure and cut an 8" length of 24-gauge floral wire.

② Pinch the ribbon about 8" from one end.

③ With the long end of the ribbon, form a loop approximately 4". Twist the ribbon under your thumb and forefinger.

④ Continue pinching the ribbon and create a second loop on the opposite side.

⑤ Repeat this process until you have the desired even number of loops on either side of the center. Secure the loops by inserting an 8" length of 24-gauge floral wire through the center and twisting the wire securely.

⑥ Cut the tails to an 8" length.

⑦ Using your other color ribbon, make a second bow following the above directions, but making the loops slightly smaller than the first bow. This will ensure that all loops are visible.

⑧ Insert the second bow into the center of the first bow, securely twisting the floral wire from both bows together.

⑨ Adjust the loops and finish the tails as desired.

HOW TO MAKE A CURLING RIBBON BOW

Curly-Q

Curling ribbon bows are fast and easy. With the natural tendency of the ribbon to curl on its own, adding a quick flick along the edge with the scissors makes the ribbon curl like beautiful ringlets.

Instructions:

① Measure and cut four 4' lengths of different colored curling ribbon.

② Gather the three lengths together. Fold in half three times and staple them together at the fold.

③ Pinch the stapled ribbons together and secure with a piece of Scotch Tape wrapped around the top. Cut the ends of the ribbon lengths apart.

④ Hold each length of ribbon, next to the stapled end, between your thumb and forefinger.

⑤ Carefully pull one edge of the open scissors down the length of each strand of ribbon. Continue this process with each remaining length of ribbon.

⑥ Attach the bow to the package (gift). The ribbon can be attached to the package by tying it to the ribbon wrapped around the gift.

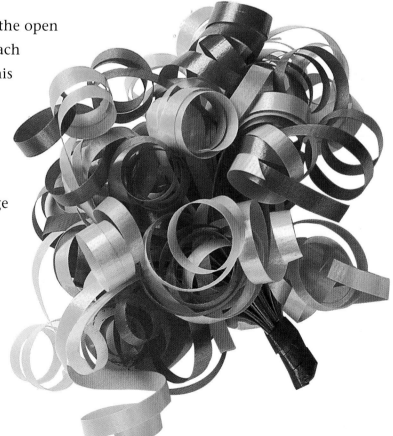

HOW TO
MAKE A SHOELACE BOW

Instructions:

① To make a shoelace bow, measure and cut 3' of ribbon.

② Fold the ribbon in half.

③ Make one 4" loop on one side of the middle fold and another 4" loop on the opposite side of the middle fold.

④ Grasp one loop in each hand and tie in a knot.

⑤ Adjust the loops and finish the tails as desired.

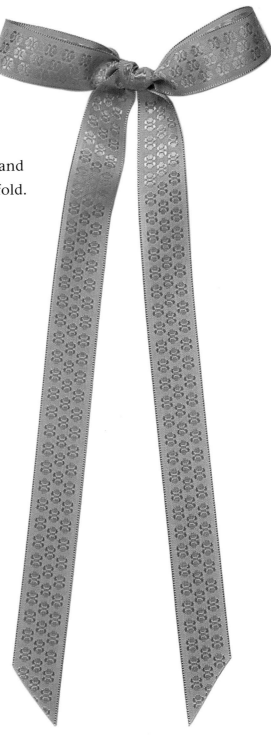

One-Two, Tie My Shoe

CHAPTER **THREE**

Wedding Bells

FLORAL **FINESSE**

Materials:

- ✢ 1 appropriate-size gift box
- ✢ 2 sheets tan tissue paper
- ✢ 1 roll gold-patterned cellophane wrap
- ✢ 12' of 1 1/2" ivory brocade ribbon
- ✢ 1 piece ivory card stock
- ✢ Winward Silk permanent botanicals:
  - • 3 stems sheer ivory rose
  - • 1 stem rose leaves
- ✢ 1 jar gold embossing powder
- ✢ 1 "Best Wishes" rubber stamp
- ✢ 1 scroll-design rubber stamp

- ✢ 1 black embossing ink pad
- ✢ 1 roll Scotch Satin Tape
- ✢ silver floral wire
- ✢ floral stem wrap
- ✢ palette paper

Tools:

- ✢ Loew-Cornell fan paintbrush
- ✢ Fiskars all-purpose scissors
- ✢ embossing heat tool
- ✢ glue gun and glue sticks
- ✢ wire cutters

Instructions:

① Wrap the gift box using the tan tissue paper. Measure and cut the cellophane wrap to fit the gift box. Wrap the box again with the cellophane. Refer to "Gift-Wrapping Basics: How to wrap a box."

② Use the wire cutters to cut the three rose stems and the one rose leaf stem approximately 18" in length.

③ Measure and cut a 2" piece of floral wire.

④ Gather the three rose stems together. Place the rose leaf stem behind the roses. Wrap the piece of wire around the four stems at the lowest leaf point and twist the wire to secure the stems in place.

⑤ Adhere the end of the floral stem wrap over the wire. Begin gently pulling and wrapping the tape around the stems, overlapping as you go, allowing the wrap to adhere to itself. Continue down the stems until you reach the bottom. Tear some wrap from the roll and adhere the wrap to itself.

⑥ Use the scissors to cut a 21" piece of ribbon. Apply a small dot of glue to one end of the ribbon. Adhere that end of the ribbon approximately 1/2" up from the bottom back of the stems, vertically. Draw the ribbon down over the end of the stems and up to the front. Twist the ribbon and begin wrapping the ribbon around the stems in an upward and angled direction to the top of the stems, finishing with the ribbon at the back. Cut any excess ribbon, allowing 1/4" for a finishing fold. Adhere the ribbon to the stem with a small dot of glue.

⑦ Tie the remaining length of ribbon around the stem with a shoelace bow. Refer to "Bow-Making: How to make a shoelace bow."

⑧ Run a bead of glue down the back of the stems and place the flowers on the top of the gift box, angled to diagonally opposite corners.

⑨ Glue the tails of the ribbon randomly to the gift box, allowing the ribbon to loop. Use the scissors to cut an inverted "V" at the ends of the ribbon tails.

GIFT TAG IDEA

1. Measure and cut a 3" x 5" piece of ivory card stock.
2. Place the sheet of palette paper on the workspace. Place the gift card on the palette paper.
3. Load the scroll stamp liberally with the black ink, keeping the edges of the stamp clean. Quickly place the stamp on the top right corner of the card approximately 1/8" from the edge. Immediately sprinkle the gold embossing powder over the ink, completely covering the stamped impression. Tap the excess embossing powder from the card. Using the soft fan brush, carefully dust any powder from the remaining card area.
4. Move the card to a separate workplace. Holding the embossing heat tool approximately 12" from the card, apply heat to the stamped image until the powder melts and becomes shiny. Be careful not to burn the paper. Repeat this process on all four corners of the card.
5. Load the "Best Wishes" stamp liberally with the black ink, keeping the edges of the stamp clean. Repeat the process above, embossing the "Best Wishes" stamp close to the top right-hand corner. Write your message in the lower left-hand corner of the card.
6. Carefully pour the remaining embossing power from the palette paper back into the jar.

PEEK-A-BOO

Materials:

+ 1 gift box
+ 1 roll white craft paper
+ 1 wedding-bell-themed stencil
+ 1 package gold tissue paper
+ 1 roll 6" gold-fleck white tulle
+ 6' of 2" white filmy ribbon with gold trim
+ 1 package white bell confetti
+ 1 can 3M Spray Mount
+ 1 Scotch Pop-up Tape Strip Dispenser
+ 1 roll Scotch Double-Stick Tape
+ 1 Scotch Permanent Adhesive Glue Stick
+ paper towels

Tools:

+ Fiskars all-purpose scissors
+ Fiskars personal paper trimmer
+ Fiskars self-healing mat
+ Fiskars acrylic ruler
+ X-Acto knife
+ pencil
+ eraser
+ paper-piercing tool

GIFT TAG IDEA

1. Using a paper trimmer, cut a piece of white craft paper to measure 10" x 6".
2. Fold the paper in half to create a card.
3. Tear a piece of gold tissue paper to fit the front of the card and adhere the tissue using a glue stick.
4. Following the same technique as above, stencil and pierce a set of bells. Cut the bells out, leaving a 1/4" border around the piercing. Center and adhere the bells on the gold tissue paper.
5. Open the card and personalize with your wedding wishes. Tuck the card under some of the wrapped tulle.

Package #2

This smaller gift box was wrapped using the same technique, but on a simpler scale.

Instructions:

① Measure and cut enough white craft paper to fit the gift box. Allow sufficient paper to make a crisp fold and to neatly finish the ends of the package. Without taping, wrap the gift temporarily, following "Gift-Wrapping Basics: How to wrap a box." Make all the creases on the paper as if you were wrapping it permanently. Unwrap the gift and place the white craft paper right-side down on a flat surface.

② Determine by the creases the area of the gift-wrap that will cover the top of the box. Place six stacked sheets of paper towel under this area.

③ Spray a light coat of spray mount to the back side of the stencil. Position the stencil on an angle in the upper left-hand corner of this area. Use the pencil to trace the bottom of the bell stencil. This area will not be pierced.

④ Leaving the stencil in place, use the paper-piercing tool to pierce a series of close holes along the interior lines of the stencil. Repeat the same process on the other three corners of the same area of the paper. Repeat this process on other areas of the paper. Ensure that the paper towel is under the areas you are piercing.

⑤ Remove the paper towel and replace it with the cutting mat. Using the X-Acto knife, cut out all bottoms of the bells and erase any pencil lines. Turn the paper over. This is the right side.

⑥ Referring to "Gift-Wrapping Basics: How to wrap a box," first wrap the box in gold tissue paper, then rewrap the gift on the pierced paper, ensuring that you position it following the original creases. The gold tissue paper will show through the areas that are cut and pierced.

⑦ Wrap tulle tightly around all four sides of the box, ending up, on top, with a knot. Tie a shoelace bow. Refer to "Bow-Making: How to make a shoelace bow."

⑧ Cut the ends of the tulle to leave 12", and tie a knot in each end. Insert several of the white bell confetti under the tightly tied tulle on the package and into the ends of the two tulle tails.

⑨ Tie another shoelace bow with 3' of the filmy white ribbon and attach it to the middle of the tulle bow. Trim the ends of the ribbon with an inverted "V" cut and tie them off in a knot.

CORDIALLY **INVITED**

Materials:

✣ 1 gift box
✣ 2 sheets light-colored
   tissue paper
✣ 9' of 1 1/4" white florist
   satin ribbon
✣ 1 roll narrow white
   Spool O' Ribbon
✣ 1 can white webbing
   spray
✣ 1 small wedding
   rubber stamp
   of choice
✣ 1 wedding
   invitation
✣ 1 brown ink
   pad
✣ 1 Scotch
   Permanent
   Adhesive
   Glue
   Stick
✣ 1 Scotch
   Pop-up
   Satin Tape
   Dispenser
✣ 1 roll Scotch Double-
   Stick Tape
✣ large trash bag
✣ palette paper

Tools:

✣ Fiskars all-purpose scissors
✣ glue gun and glue sticks

Instructions:

① Protect a flat work surface with an open trash bag. Place the two sheets of tissue paper one on top of the other.

② In a well-ventilated area, randomly spray the tissue with the webbing spray, following manufacturer's instructions. Let the webbing spray dry completely.

③ To wrap the gift box, follow the instructions under "Gift-Wrapping Basics: How to wrap a box."

④ Place the white satin ribbon, shiny-side up, on a piece of palette paper. Stamp the ribbon using the wedding stamp and brown ink, beginning at one end of the ribbon, leaving approximately 3" between each image.

⑤ To make a six-point bow using the stamped ribbon, refer to "Bow-Making: How to make a six-point bow." Instead of wiring the bow, use a 3' length of white Spool O' Ribbon to tie the center of the bow securely. Allow the remaining ribbon to drape from the bow.

⑥ Apply a piece of double-stick tape to the back of the wedding invitation. Adhere the invitation to the middle of the gift box.

⑦ Apply a dot of glue to the bow and adhere the bow to the top of the invitation. Allow the narrow ribbon tails to drape over the wedding invitation – and the stamped ribbon to sit under the invitation.

⑧ Use the scissors to cut an inverted "V" in the tails of the ribbon.

GIFT TAG IDEA

Very often, the bride and groom wind up without an invitation as a keepsake! This technique gives them a wonderful memento to frame or simply keep for years to come. You can also tailor the gift-wrapping to the style of the invitation, by incorporating one aspect of the invitation on the wrapping paper, such as lace or a rose. It will be much appreciated.

LOVE & **LACE**

Materials:

- ✣ 1 gift box
- ✣ 1 square cutwork lace tablecloth
- ✣ 1 cutwork lace table runner
- ✣ 4 sheets floral-print tissue paper
- ✣ 3' of 2 1/4" ivory voile ribbon
- ✣ 9' of 6" ivory tulle
- ✣ Spool O' Ribbon:
  - • 1 roll narrow ivory
  - • 1 roll narrow ivory picot edge
  - • 1 roll narrow melon
  - • 1 roll narrow melon picot edge
- ✣ 1 bottle DecoArt Dazzling Metallics, Glorious Gold acrylic paint
- ✣ 1 wedding motif rubber stamp
- ✣ white note card
- ✣ 1 stem Winward Silk Florals, cymbidium orchid peach
- ✣ 1 roll Scotch Satin Tape
- ✣ palette paper
- ✣ wedge sponge
- ✣ straight pins

Tools:

- ✣ Fiskars all-purpose scissors
- ✣ Fiskars circle hand punch
- ✣ wire cutters

Instructions:

① Wrap the gift box with the tissue paper, referring to "Basic Gift-Wrapping: How to wrap a box."

② Lay the square lace tablecloth right-side down on a flat work surface.

③ Place the wrapped gift box right-side up on the work surface. Wrap the sides of the box with the tablecloth as you would with paper, securing the tablecloth in place with straight pins. Turn the box right-side up.

④ Find the center of the 9' of ivory tulle. Place the center of the tulle in the center of the top of the box.

Wrap the tulle down the sides, criss-crossing it across the bottom and back up the opposite sides of the box, finishing on the top with a knot and leaving the ends trailing over the edges of the box. Remove the pins.

⑤ To create the table-runner bow, begin at one end of the runner and fold over 3". Continue folding the runner back and forth, pleating it like a fan until you reach the end.

⑥ Place the pleated runner on top of the tulle knot. Draw the two ends of the tulle around the center of the runner and tie a shoelace bow. Allow the remaining tulle to drape over the edges of the box.

⑦ Use the wire cutters to cut the orchid stem to approximately 22".

⑧ Place the stem under the tulle on the top of the box, flush with the tablecloth.

⑨ Cut a 12" length of the voile ribbon. Feed this piece of ribbon under the tulle and orchid and tie the ribbon in a knot.

⑩ Cut a 24" length of each of the narrow ribbons. Gather the four ribbons together, feed one end under the orchid and tulle, and tie the ribbons in a knot.

⑪ Allow the ends of all ribbons to drape over the sides of the box.

⑫ Gently pull the sides of the tablecloth around the top of the box, making sure the edges are raised about 1/4" from the edges, and the side folds are neat.

⑬ Gently separate the accordion folds of the table runner to create a soft look.

This is a fabulous wrapping idea if your gift to the bride and groom is a set of dishes or silverware. Including the tablecloth, table runner and floral stem as part of the gift provides a ready-made table setting, preparing them to entertain their first guests!

GIFT TAG IDEA

1. Squeeze a puddle of gold paint on the palette paper.
2. Dip the wedding stamp in the gold paint.
3. Carefully place the stamp on the top of the note card, apply gentle pressure, and remove the stamp to reveal the motif. Let the paint dry completely.
4. Punch a hole in the top left corner of the card. Feed one end of one of the ribbon tails through the hole in the card, and draw the card up to the top of the gift.

EMBOSSED **KEEPSAKE**

Materials:

✣ 1 gift box

✣ 1 roll white, textured wallpaper

✣ 9' of 3" wired ribbon, white

✣ 1 package Paragon ArtEmboss Metal – light brass

✣ ArtEmboss tracing patterns – 1 tracing monogram

✣ 1 tracing alphabet

✣ 1 Sharpie Fine Point Black Permanent Marker

✣ paper towels

Tools:

✣ Fiskars 2-piece Home & Office Scissor

✣ Fiskars circle hand punch Set (includes a small pair of scissors and a regular pair)

✣ glue gun and glue sticks

GIFT TAG IDEA

Given that part of the decorating of these packages includes metal tags, use this to your advantage. Using a permanent marker, write your message on the back of one of the tags. The couple can keep the tag and perhaps use it as a Christmas decoration in the future.

Instructions:

① Measure and cut the wallpaper to fit the gift box.

② To wrap the box, refer to "Gift-Wrapping Basics: How to wrap a box." Due to the thickness of the wallpaper, use a glue gun to adhere the edges of the paper by placing a bead of glue on the wrong side of the paper and adhering it to the box.

③ Place four sheets of paper towel on a flat work surface. Place the brass metal sheet on the paper towel.

④ Place the tracing monogram on the metal sheet, singling out the rectangle shape. Following manufacturer's instructions, emboss the rectangle shape.

⑤ Use the small scissors to carefully cut around the rectangle.

⑥ In the same manner, emboss the bride and groom's initials on the front of the rectangle, using the tracing alphabet.

⑦ Use the punch to make a hole in the top center of the metal rectangle.

⑧ Place the ribbon flat on the work surface. Place the gift box right-side down, horizontally, on top of the ribbon. Bring the ends of the ribbon up and over the ends of the box, criss-crossing it in the middle of the back of the box. Flip the box right-side up and bring the ribbon up and over the sides of the box. Tie a knot. Finish by tying a shoelace bow. Refer to "Bow-Making: How to make a shoelace bow."

⑨ Feed the ends of the bow tails through the hole in the tag, from the front to the back. Gently pull the tails until the tag rests against the bow.

⑩ Use the larger scissors to cut an inverted "V" in the ends of the ribbon.

Package #2

Embossed metal makes a fabulous impact, especially on gifts. Simply finishing a gift box with beautiful ribbons and attaching a specially embossed tag to enhance the gift will impress the bride and groom.

Materials:

- 1 11″ glass hurricane lamp
- 2 sheets silver tissue paper
- 1 bottle Armour Etch Glass Etching Cream
- 9′ of 2 1/4″ white woven ribbon
- Spool O' Ribbon:
    - 1 roll narrow white
    - 1 roll white picot edge
- 1 sheet adhesive-backed wedding die cuts
- 1 10″ x 20″ clear cello bag
- 1 5″ x 10″ clear cello bag
- 1 can 3M PhotoMount Adhesive
- 1 Scotch Permanent Adhesive Glue Stick
- 1 roll Scotch Long-Mask Masking Tape

- 1 Painter's Metallic Paint Marker, Medium Silver
- plain white paper
- white note card
- paper towels
- water
- disposable latex gloves

Tools:

- Loew-Cornell small foam brush
- Fiskars all-purpose scissors
- Fiskars circle hand punch
- Fiskars plain brayer
- Fiskars paper edgers – heartstrings
- pencil

Instructions:

① Use the scissors to carefully cut around the die-cut image you choose to use on the center of the hurricane lamp, leaving as much space around the image as you can.

② Remove the middle image of the die cut from the backing and set aside.

③ Place the hurricane lamp on its side. Adhere the die-cut image as a template on the center of the hurricane and secure all edges with masking tape.

④ Wearing disposable latex gloves, use the foam brush to apply the etching cream to the die-cut image only. Leave the etching cream on for approximately one minute.

⑤ Following manufacturer's instructions, carefully rinse the etching cream from the hurricane lamp under warm running water. The template will detach from the glass when wet. Dry the hurricane lamp with a paper towel. Wash the foam brush and blot it dry on a paper towel.

⑥ Gently scrunch one sheet of silver tissue paper in the middle and insert it into one end of the hurricane lamp. Repeat with the second piece of tissue paper for the opposite end of the hurricane lamp.

⑦ Cut away the bottom edge of the 10" x 20" clear cello bag. Open the bag and insert the hurricane lamp lengthwise into the center.

⑧ Cut the 9' of 2 1/4" woven ribbon in half. Tie one piece around each end of the hurricane lamp, tying a simple shoelace bow. Refer to "Bow-Making: How to make a shoelace bow."

⑨ Cut two 12" lengths of each of the narrow and picot-edge Spool O' Ribbon. Tie one 12" piece of narrow and one 12" piece of picot ribbon around each end of the hurricane lamp, tying a shoelace bow over the woven ribbon bow.

PACKAGE #2

Etching is a fantastic way to personalize a special gift. Small glass votives are particularly pretty when done this way. They

can provide that extra punch when making small "thinking of you" gifts to give to the guests at a wedding. This time, place the actual die-cut image, a smaller one for this smaller project, on the votive. Etch the entire votive, wash the etching cream away and remove the die-cut image. The votive will be completely etched other than the small die-cut image. Finish by placing the votive in the 5" x 10" clear cello bag and decorate with pretty ribbon and bows.

GIFT TAG IDEA

1. Using the die-cut images as tracers, cut an image from the silver tissue paper.
2. In a well-ventilated area, lightly spray the back of the tissue-paper image with the spray-mount adhesive. Quickly adhere it to the front of a note card. Gently roll over the image with the brayer to remove any air bubbles.
3. Measure in 1/4" from the open edge of the front of the card and pencil a line across the card. Using the paper edgers, cut along the pencil line. Run the silver pen along the decorative edge created by the paper edgers.
4. On the inside edge of the back of the card, adhere a piece of white picot Spool O' Ribbon, using the glue stick.
5. Using any scraps of cello, cover the top front of the note card to protect the image.
6. Use the punch to make a hole through the card, in the top left corner.
7. Cut a 6" piece of narrow ribbon. Feed one end of the ribbon through the hole and secure it to the bow on one end of the hurricane lamp.

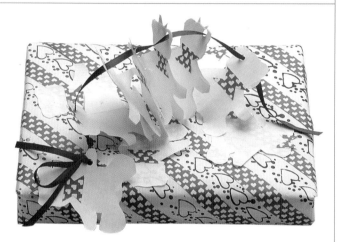

CHAPTER **FOUR**

Baby Arrives

TEDDY BEAR **PICNIC**

Materials:

+ 1 roll white craft paper
+ 8' of white cording
+ 1 pkg. Daisy Kingdom Chenille Snuggles Wallies (or wallpaper cutouts of your choice)
+ 1 bottle DecoArt Americana Mint Julep Green acrylic paint
+ 1 Scotch Pop-up Tape Strip Dispenser
+ 1 Scotch Permanent Adhesive Glue Stick
+ palette paper
+ paper towels
+ water container

Tools:

+ Fiskars all-purpose scissors
+ Fiskars circle hand punch
+ Fiskars acrylic ruler
+ small sponge
+ glue gun and glue sticks

Instructions:

① Measure and cut the craft paper to fit the gift box. Allow enough for a crisp fold and to neatly finish the ends of the package.

② Place a puddle of the Mint Julep Green paint on the palette paper. Moisten the small sponge with water and squeeze any excess out with a paper towel.

③ Lay the craft paper flat on the work surface, right-side up. Begin lightly sponging the green paint on the craft paper in an overall pattern. Allow the paint to dry completely. Wash the sponge and blot it dry on a paper towel.

④ Arrange the various Wallies cutouts on the craft paper in a pleasing manner.

⑤ Using the glue stick, adhere each cutout on to the craft paper, setting aside three cutouts: two for the bow and one for the gift tag.

⑥ To wrap the gift, refer to "Gift-Wrapping Basics: How to wrap a box."

⑦ To make the bow, lay the white cording out flat on the work surface. Lay the box upside down, lengthwise, on the center point of the cord. Draw the pieces of cording over the ends of the box to the center, and loop the cording over and under. Turn the box counter clockwise and draw the cording around the sides of the box. Turn the box over and tie the cording securely in the middle of the top of the box, embellishing with a shoelace bow. Refer to "Bow-Making: How to make a shoelace bow." Adjust each loop of the bow to hold one cutout each.

⑧ Using the glue gun, apply a thin strip of glue from top to bottom in the center of one cutout pattern. Glue the cutout on one loop of the bow, gently bending to follow the curve of the loop. Apply the second cutout to the second loop in the same manner.

GIFT TAG IDEA

1. To make a coordinating gift tag, use the glue stick to attach one cutout on a piece of craft paper.
2. Use the scissors to carefully cut around the pattern.
3. Using the punch, make a hole at the top of the cutout.
4. Thread one end of the cording from the bow through the hole and position the cutout close to the bow. Tie the ends of the cording tails in a knot.

PACKAGE #2

To make gift-wrap unique to a baby boy, incorporate large-cloud Wallies cutouts on blue tissue paper. Use the same wrapping technique as above, placing the bears as though they are floating on the clouds.

PACKAGE #3

If the new bundle of joy is a girl, vellum bags are just the thing to celebrate her arrival. Continuing with the theme of using wallpaper cutouts, glue two cutouts to the front of a plain velum bag. Dressed up with pink tissue, a pretty tulle bow and a chenille stem, your design will enhance the perfect gift.

DANCING **BEARS**

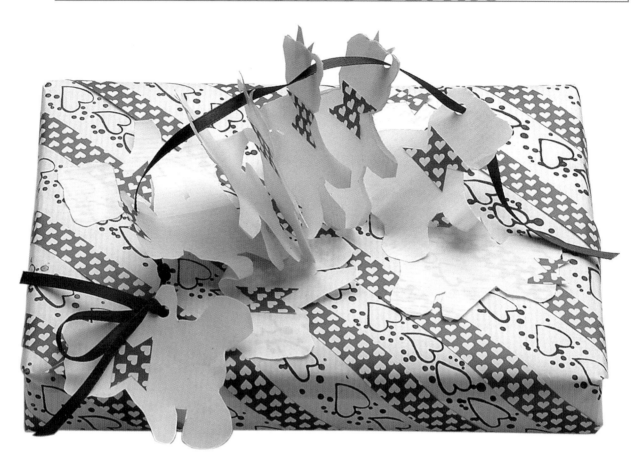

Materials:

✤ 1 roll white craft paper

✤ 1 12″ x 12″ sheet Fiskars Photo
Memories Red and White Hearts
(or memory paper of your choice)

✤ 1 bottle DecoArt Americana Tomato
Red acrylic paint

✤ 1 roll 1/8″ red Spool O' Ribbon

✤ Teddy bear cutout pattern or pattern
of your choice

✤ 1 roll Scotch Satin Tape

✤ 1 Scotch Permanent Adhesive
Glue Stick

✤ palette paper

✤ water container

✤ paper towels

Tools:

✤ Fiskars all-purpose scissors

✤ Fiskars rotary cutter

✤ Fiskars self-healing mat

✤ Fiskars acrylic ruler

✤ Fiskars circle hand punch

✤ Plaid Fun-to-Paint Heart Mini Roller

Instructions:

① Measure and cut the craft paper to fit your gift box. Allow enough for a crisp fold and to neatly finish the ends of the package.

② Lay the sheet of hearts memory paper flat on the self-healing mat, right-side up.

③ Place a ruler, corner to corner, across the paper. Using the rotary cutter, begin cutting strips of equal width (approximately 3/4") until the full sheet has been cut.

④ Place the sheet of craft paper on the work surface, right-side up. Using the glue stick, adhere the longest strip of hearts memory paper to the middle of the sheet of craft paper, on a diagonal. Continue adhering the strips of hearts memory paper in the order in which they were cut, working up from the first piece and down from the first piece, leaving approximately 1 1/2" between each strip, until all but one strip is used up. Set the unused strip aside.

⑤ Squeeze a puddle of Tomato Red acrylic paint on the palette paper. Carefully roll the Heart Mini Roller across the paint. Roll off excess paint on the palette paper.

⑥ Beginning at one corner, carefully roll the heart pattern between the strips of hearts memory paper. Reapply the paint and continue rolling the hearts until the sheet is covered. Let the paint dry completely. Wash the heart roller and blot it dry on a paper towel.

⑦ To wrap the box, refer to "Gift-Wrapping Basics: How to wrap a box."

⑧ To make the "Dancing Bears," use the scissors to cut a strip of white craft paper approximately 36" in length and of a height to accommodate the teddy bear pattern.

⑨ Lay the strip horizontally on the work surface. Place the teddy bear pattern vertically at one end of the strip of paper and trace around the shape.

⑩ Remove the pattern and begin folding the paper back and forth, in a fan manner, with the teddy bear image facing you. Ensure that the hands of the bear pattern are against the folds of the paper.

⑪ When the paper is completely folded, carefully cut around the pattern, being sure not to cut the edge of the bears' hands. Spread the pattern out. The bears should be joined at the hands.

⑫ Cut two strips of three bears each from the main strip of bears. Set the main strip of bears aside.

GIFT TAG IDEA

1. To make a coordinating gift tag, trace the teddy bear pattern onto a piece of craft paper.
2. Use the glue stick to attach the teddy bear to a second piece of craft paper.
3. Carefully cut the bear out.
4. Punch a hole in one hand of the bear.
5. Use the existing ribbon tails to tie the gift tag to the gift.

⑬ Using the glue stick, apply glue to the ends of one of the three 'cut' bear strips. Adhere the bears on one end of the box, on an angle, allowing the middle bear to be raised off the paper. Repeat with the second three-bear strip at the opposite end of the box.

⑭ To place the main strip of bears, apply glue to the first bear and adhere it to the second bear. Continue adhering two bears together down the chain, until complete.

⑮ Using the punch, make a hole in the opposite ears of each set of bears until all have been punched, including the two raised bears on the package.

⑯ Cut a length of the red Spool O' Ribbon long enough to thread through the holes – and allow extra at each end. Start with a raised bear on one end and thread the ribbon through the bear's ears. When you reach the end, stand the strip of bears up on the box, gently separating them to allow them to "dance." Tie a small knot at the ends of the ribbon.

PACKAGE #2

Including part of the gift in the wrapping is fun and gives the recipient an idea of what might be inside. Using dimensional paint to make your own design on shiny wrapping paper is not only easy, but provides a great new look for gift-wrapping for babies. Incorporating small baby face cloths, a soft tulle bow and your own personally designed gift tag will be truly impressive.

PACKAGE #3

Nothing personalizes a gift more than your own handwriting. Using a felt pen and a scrawling handwriting, write "baby" over simple white craft paper. The addition of some pretty curling ribbon and a sweet, soft toy tucked into the bow completes this unique look.

BABIES ARE **SUNSHINE**

Materials:

- 1 roll white craft paper
- 1 package yellow tissue paper
- 1 bottle DecoArt Americana Yellow Light acrylic paint
- Plaid Simply Stamps Baby
- Plaid Dimensional fabric paint:
  - 1 bottle Yellow Pearl
  - 1 bottle White Pearl
- 16' of white grosgrain ribbon
- Spool O' Ribbon:
  - 1 roll narrow yellow
  - 1 roll narrow white
  - 1 roll narrow yellow wired ribbon
- 1 small bottle bleach
- 1 Scotch Pop-up Tape Strip Dispenser
- 1 Scotch Permanent Adhesive Glue Stick
- silver floral wire
- disposable latex gloves
- palette paper
- water container
- paper towels

Tools:

- Fiskars all-purpose scissors
- Fiskars acrylic ruler
- Fiskars circle hand punch
- small glass bowl
- small wedge sponge
- wire cutters
- pencil

Instructions:

① Lay a sheet of yellow tissue paper on a flat work surface.

② Mix approximately two teaspoons of bleach to 1/2 cup water in a glass mixing bowl. Be sure to wear disposable latex gloves.

③ Separate the baby stamps. Dip one small stamp into the bleach solution and gently tap off any excess.

④ Carefully press the stamp onto the yellow tissue paper. Continue dipping the stamp in the bleach solution and stamping on the tissue paper in a random pattern. The bleach will lift the color of the tissue paper. Let the tissue dry completely. Wash the stamp and blot it dry on a paper towel.

⑤ Outline the individual stamp motifs with White Pearl dimensional fabric paint. Let the paint dry completely.

⑥ Line the yellow tissue paper with one sheet of white tissue paper. To wrap the gift, refer to "Gift-Wrapping Basics: How to wrap a box."

⑦ Cut a 15' length of white grosgrain ribbon. Lay the ribbon flat on the work surface.

⑧ Place a small puddle of Yellow Light paint on the palette paper. Apply paint to a second small-baby stamp motif using the wedge sponge. Beginning at one end of the ribbon, stamp images along the length of the ribbon, reapplying paint as you need it. Let the paint dry completely. Wash the sponge and stamp and blot them dry on a paper towel.

⑨ To make the bow, lay the ribbon right-side down on the work surface. Lay the box upside down, lengthwise, on the center of the ribbon. Draw the pieces of ribbon around the ends of the box to the center and loop the ribbon over and under. Turn the box counter clockwise and draw the two lengths of ribbon around the sides of the box. Turn the box over and tie the ribbon in a knot in the center of the top of the box.

⑩ Using the wire cutters, cut a 2" piece of floral wire. Hold the two ribbon lengths together in one hand. While holding the loop snug against the knot, begin looping the remaining ribbon back and forth in a figure-eight motion to make a six-point bow. Refer to "Bow-Making: How to make a six-point bow." Keep the loops

GIFT TAG IDEA

1. Enlarge the baby motif pattern and trace the pattern onto a piece of white craft paper.
2. Carefully cut around the pattern.
3. Trace around the edge of the motif with Yellow Pearl dimensional fabric paint and let the paint dry completely.
4. Punch a hole in the top of the baby-motif card.
5. Thread one length of yellow ribbon through the hole in the gift tag and place the tag at the bottom of the bow. Tie a small knot to secure the tag to the ribbon.

even and keep the right sides of the ribbon out, leaving enough for the ties. Make a small loop in the middle and insert a piece of florist wire through the center of the bow and under the knot. Twist the wire securely.

⑪ Gently separate the loops of the bow. Use the scissors to cut an inverted "V" in the ribbon tails.

⑫ Cut a 12" length of each of the yellow and white Spool O' Ribbons. Thread the ribbon under the knot and tie a shoelace bow. Refer to "Bow-Making: How to make a shoelace bow."

PACKAGE #2

Bleach is an easy and inexpensive material to use. By applying this interesting technique, you can reverse the pattern by stamping baby motifs in yellow acrylic paint on white tissue paper. Coordinate the ribbon by bleaching the baby motif on

yellow ribbon and out-lining each motif with white dimensional paint. This is particularly eye-catching when you have more than one gift.

PACKAGE #3

If time is short and nothing in your wrapping-paper stash fits the baby bill, plastic tablecloths are the perfect answer. Wrap the gift in a plastic tablecloth, finish with

pretty tulle and diaper pins attached to the center of the bow, along with a few strands of yellow Spool O' Ribbon. You'll give a fabulous look to your gift package.

RATTLED

Materials:

+ 1 baby bath-toy set, with mesh bag and decorative suction cups
+ assortment of baby-bath toys, face cloths, bath books, comb and brush
+ 1 small rattle
+ 1 pacifier
+ 1 pair baby nail clippers
+ 1 baby toothbrush
+ 1 small baby-bottle brush

+ 1 roll narrow, white, picot-edge Spool O' Ribbon
+ baby stickers
+ shaped 3M Post-It Notes
+ 1 Scotch Permanent Adhesive Glue Stick

Tools:

+ Fiskars all-purpose scissors
+ Fiskars circle hand punch

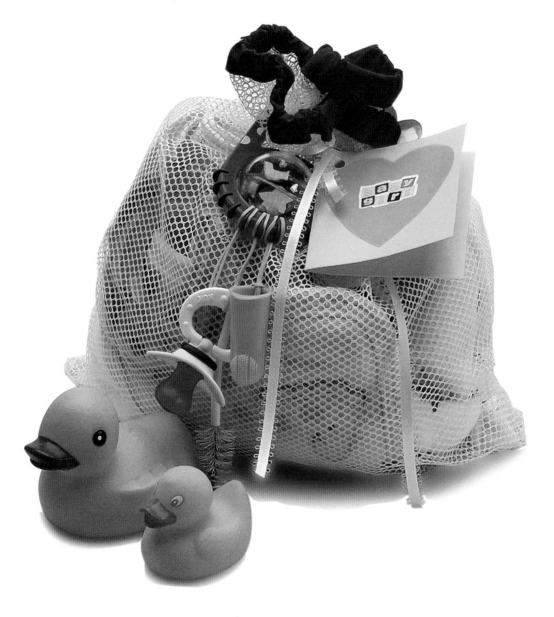

Instructions:

① Remove all tags and price tickets from the baby bath toys, face cloths, bath books and other assorted baby items.

② Using the bath-toy mesh bag as the wrapping for the gift, insert the assortment of baby bath toys, face cloths, bath books, and comb and brush into the mesh bag in a pleasing manner.

③ Using the scissors, cut a piece of the white picot ribbon approximately 24" in length. Wrap the ribbon around the top of the mesh bag and tie the ribbon in a shoelace bow. Refer to "Bow-Making: How to make a shoelace bow."

④ Attach the decorative suction cups to the bag at the top.

⑤ To create the rattle decoration, use small pieces of ribbon to attach the pacifier, baby-bottle brush, baby toothbrush, and baby nail clippers to the rattle, so the small items hang from the rattle.

⑥ Attach the rattle to the top of the mesh bag.

GIFT TAG IDEA

1. Cut a piece of colored paper approximately 5" x 2 1/2".
2. Fold the paper in half.
3. Adhere a shaped 3M Post-It Note to the front of the folded card, using a glue stick.
4. Punch a hole in the upper left-hand corner of the card.
5. Apply an appropriate baby sticker to the middle of the center image.
6. Loop the white picot ribbon through the hole in the card and tie a shoelace bow.
7. Attach the card to the top of the mesh bag.

This is a great gift to give at a shower. The idea of creating the rattle – with all the little baby items hanging from it – encourages the mom-to-be to join in on the fun and wear the rattle during the shower. This idea was passed along to me from my friend, Gerry, and I thought it was such a great idea, I had to incorporate it in this book. Thanks Gerry!

BRIGHT COMPANIONS

Materials:

✣ Colorful baby swimwear diapers, either washable or disposable
✣ 1 package of bright and mixed-color photography paper
✣ 1 package brightly colored balloons
✣ 1 package balloon sticks
✣ 6 - 8 bottles baby food for each swimwear diaper
✣ 1 Scotch Permanent Adhesive Glue Stick

Tools:

✣ Fiskars all-purpose scissors
✣ Fiskars paper crimper
✣ Fiskars circle hand punch
✣ paper shredder

Instructions:

① Open the swimwear diapers up and tie them off at the front, as shown in the photograph.

② To create colorful paper-shred, cut several sheets of pink, yellow, green and purple photocopy paper in half.

③ Run each half-sheet of paper through the paper crimper, one at a time.

④ Feed two or three half-sheets of crimped paper through the paper shredder to create long strips.

⑤ Remove the strips from the paper shredder. Mix the paper thoroughly and squeeze handfuls of the paper shred to crumple the paper further.

⑥ Insert handfuls of paper-shred into each of the swimwear diapers.

⑦ Nestle jars of baby food and baby juice into the diapers, arranging the jars in a pleasing manner.

⑧ Inflate three balloons for each of the diapers. Attach each balloon to a balloon stick.

⑨ Insert the balloons into the middle of the diapers.

⑩ Make several of these centerpieces and place one in the middle of each table at the baby shower. Mom can take these centerpieces home and use both the diapers and the baby food.

GIFT TAG IDEA

1. Trace a favorite shape, perhaps a heart, onto a piece of brightly colored photocopy paper and cut the shape out.
2. Cut a second, smaller heart from a different colored paper, and a third heart, smaller still, from a third colored paper.
3. Stack and glue the heart shapes in accordance with their size, and write your message on the top heart.
4. Punch a hole at the top of the heart, and attach it to the diaper, either with a small piece of ribbon, the pull-ties at the front of the diapers, or a diaper pin.

PRIMARY COLORS

Materials:

- ✢ 1 package red tissue paper
- ✢ 1 roll clear cello wrap
- ✢ Rubber Stampede curveDecor:
  - • Happy Butterfly
- ✢ 1 Rubber Stampede curveDecor handle
- ✢ DecoArt Americana acrylic paint:
  - • 1 bottle Yellow Light
  - • 1 bottle True Red
  - • 1 bottle Ultra Blue Deep
  - • 1 bottle Leaf Green
- ✢ 1 Plaid Simply Stamps Baby
- ✢ curling ribbon:
  - • 1 roll red
  - • 1 roll green
  - • 1 roll yellow
  - • 1 roll blue
- ✢ white note cards
- ✢ several baby-motif rubber stamps
- ✢ 1 Scotch Permanent Adhesive Glue Stick
- ✢ 1 Scotch Pop-up Tape Strip Dispenser
- ✢ water container
- ✢ palette paper
- ✢ paper towels

Tools:

- ✢ small wedge sponges
- ✢ glue gun and glue sticks

Instructions:

① Using the scissors, cut one piece of cello wrap the size of a single sheet of tissue paper.

② Place the cello wrap flat on the work surface. Following manufacturer's directions, attach the curveDecor Happy Butterfly stamp to the curveDecor handle.

③ Squeeze a puddle of Yellow Light paint on a piece of palette paper.

④ Using one of the wedge sponges, lightly apply the yellow paint to the stamp. Using a light rocking motion, press the stamp onto the cello wrap carefully, to avoid sliding. Continue stamping the cello wrap with butterfly motifs in a random manner.

⑤ Use the wedge sponge to apply the Yellow Light paint to a baby-motif stamp. Apply the stamp to the cello wrap around each butterfly. Let the paint dry completely. Wash the stamps and sponge and blot them dry on a paper towel.

⑥ Place the cello wrap, stamped-side up, flat on the work surface. Place one sheet of red tissue paper on top of the stamped pattern. To wrap the gift, refer to "Gift-Wrapping Basics: How to wrap a box."

⑦ Cut one 6' length each of the curling ribbons. Place one end of each length together and tape it to the edge of the work surface. Begin braiding the ribbon and tie a knot at the end. Remove the braid from the work surface and knot the taped end.

⑧ Cut one 8" length of each of the ribbon colors. Make a loopy bow from the braided ribbon. Refer to "Bow-Making: How to make a loopy bow." Tie the 8" lengths of ribbon around the center of the bow. Attach the bow to one corner of the package using the glue stick.

GIFT TAG IDEA

1. Cut the note cards to an appropriate size for the package.
2. Squeeze a puddle of each of the four colors of paint onto the palette paper.
3. Using all four paint colors, stamp simple baby designs on the face of the note cards, creating as many gift tags as you require
4. Apply colorful curling ribbon pieces down the sides and across the top and bottom of the note cards using the glue stick.
5. Punch a hole in the upper left-hand corner of the tags and attach them to the gifts with a piece of curling ribbon.

PACKAGE #2 (yellow package)

Sometimes, keeping the wrapping simple is the best way to go. The gift-wrap stands alone without using ribbons or any other embellishments. Using various stamps and designs on cello wrap is a wonderful way to hint at what is in the box. Whatever the theme, cello wrap is an excellent way of enhancing any design.

PACKAGE #3 (blue package)

Using cello wrap over wrapping or tissue paper is a fun way to highlight patterns and give them a special sheen. Include practical items such as safety plug covers to the bow to add further distinction to the package. This idea works well, and parents will appreciate the thought!

PACKAGE #4 (green package)

Stretch your creativity further by making your own ribbon to coordinate with your wrapping design. Plain acetate ribbon is easily available and keeps the costs to a minimum. Adhere lengths of narrow curling ribbon to the acetate ribbon, using a glue stick. It's simple and can be incorporated into any color scheme.

CHAPTER **FIVE**

Kids Create

RUBBER-BAND **MAN**

Materials:

- various neon-colored photocopy papers
- various colored and patterned adhesive drawer-liner papers
- 1 package pencil cushions in bright neon colors
- 1 package end erasers in bright colors
- 1 package regular sized erasers in bright colors
- 1 package assorted rubber bands in bright colors
- 1 package neon-colored cutouts
- 1 package neon-colored sale tags on string
- 1 Scotch Pop-up Tape Strip Dispenser
- 1 roll Scotch Double-Stick Tape
- 1 Scotch Permanent Adhesive Glue Stick
- floral wire

Tools:

- Fiskars all-purpose scissors
- Fiskars acrylic ruler
- wire cutters

Instructions:

① Create a larger piece of paper by taping the two pieces of purple photocopy paper together on the wrong side.

② To wrap the box, refer to "Gift-Wrapping Basics: How to wrap a box."

③ Once the gift is wrapped, begin by placing one rubber band around the middle of the box. Place a second and third rubber band in the same direction, approximately 1/2" apart, varying the colors. Once you have applied three to four rubber bands, reverse the direction of the bands, and continue placing another three to four going in the opposite direction. Continue this process, going back and forth in different directions, until the entire box is covered with rubber bands and a plaid pattern has formed.

④ To make the bow, wire twenty rubber bands together, using a small piece of floral wire, and make a cut so the bands spray out. Attach the bow to the gift by placing another rubber band around the middle of the bow.

PACKAGE #2

① Wrap the gift using the lime-green photocopy paper. Refer to "Gift-Wrapping Basics: How to wrap a box." If necessary, attach two pieces of paper together.

② Place three blue rubber bands on each end of the box, approximately 1/2" apart.

③ Place a small piece of double stick tape on the back of a colored eraser, and stick the eraser to the middle of the box.

PACKAGE #3

① Wrap the box in a patterned adhesive drawer-liner paper. Refer to "Gift-Wrapping Basics: How to wrap a box."

② When using the adhesive drawer-liner paper, use the glue stick to finish off the ends of the packaging.

③ Using the glue stick, adhere brightly colored cutout shapes to each of the sides, top and bottom of the box.

④ To make the pencil cushion bow, cut a piece of wire approximately 6' in length. Create a figure-eight bow with the wire. You will need five loops on each side. Attach one pencil-end eraser onto one end of each of the 10 pencil cushions. Push each wire loop together and slide a pencil cushion on to each loop. Arrange the pencil cushions in a pleasing manner, to form a flower or bow.

⑤ Place the pencil-cushion bow in the middle of the top of the box. Wrap a large blue rubber band around the middle of the box, placing it over the middle of the pencil cushion bow to hold the bow in place, then another around the middle of the box, going in the opposite direction.

GIFT TAG IDEA

I was delighted to find neon-colored sale tags in my local business supply store. I thought it a great idea to use these tags as gift tags, especially on kids' gifts. Not only are they inexpensive, but also it's fun to use a product designed for one use in a different manner. Also, I love incorporating items onto a gift that the kids can use afterwards, such as erasers, and these packages certainly give you lots of great ideas to do just that!

PACKAGE #4

① Wrap the box in a brightly colored adhesive drawer-liner paper.

② Use the glue stick to adhere the sides of the paper in place.

③ Adhere three brightly colored cutouts down the front of the package.

④ Place a small piece of double-stick tape to each of three brightly colored rectangular erasers. Adhere an eraser in the middle of each of the three colored cutouts.

HAIRY **CANARY**

Materials:

- 1 large, medium and small vellum bag with top flap
- 1 large and small vellum snap-box with lid
- 1 Rubber Stampede flower stamp
- 1 Rubber Stampede starfish stamp
- DecoArt Americana acrylic paints:
  - 1 bottle Dazzling Metallics, Rose Pearl
  - 1 bottle Dazzling Metallics, White Pearl
  - 1 bottle Lemon Yellow
- 1 can matte acrylic sealer
- 6' of 1 1/2" pink filmy wired ribbon
- 14' of 1 1/2" yellow filmy wired ribbon
- 3 metallic blue hair scrunchies
- 3 metallic pink hair scrunchies
- 1 roll light blue Wraphia
- several mini flower, shell and dolphin hairclips
- 1 large metal barrette
- bright yellow and light blue tissue paper
- white card stock
- 1 roll Scotch Long-Mask Masking Tape
- paper towels
- water container
- palette paper
- silver floral wire

Tools:

- Loew-Cornell palette knife
- Fiskars all-purpose scissors
- Fiskars circle hand punch
- wedge sponge

Instructions:

PACKAGE GROUPING #1 (pink and yellow packages)

① Lay the large vellum bag flat on the work surface, right-side up. Mask off the area below the flap of the bag.

② Dip the wedge sponge into the Rose Pearl acrylic paint. Lightly dab the paint onto the flap of the bag. Allow the paint to dry. Remove the masking tape.

③ Apply Rose Pearl paint to the decorative flower stamp. Center the flower in the middle of the front of the bag. Apply the stamp, using gentle pressure. Lift the stamp to reveal the flower motif. Wash the flower stamp and wedge sponge and blot them dry on a paper towel.

④ Once the paint is dry, and in a well-ventilated area, spray a fine coat of matte spray finish to the entire bag. When the bag is dry, reassemble it.

⑤ Fold a piece of yellow tissue paper the width of the bag. Insert it into the front and around to the back of the bag, to create a beautifully colored backdrop for the vellum. Wrap the gift in yellow tissue paper and insert it carefully inside the folded tissue paper.

⑥ Cut a 24" length of pink filmy ribbon. Feed the ribbon through the holes to the front of the bag flap. Tie a shoelace bow and trim the ends of the ribbon in an inverted "V" shape. Refer to "Bow-Making: How to make a shoelace bow."

⑦ Wrap the base of the bag with two metallic blue scrunchies and one metallic pink scrunchie. Attach a mini flower hairclip to each of the three scrunchies.

⑧ To create the medium and small vellum bags as shown in the photograph, repeat the same paint and stamp techniques as above. Wrap the medium vellum bag with two scrunchies and one on top of the small vellum bag. Attach a mini flower hair-clip to each of the scrunchies. Tie the bags using filmy ribbon, and decorate the ribbon with mini hairclips.

PACKAGE GROUPING #2 (blue and yellow packages)

① Lay the large snap vellum box and lid flat on the work surface, right-side up.

② Use the palette knife to mix equal amounts of White Pearl and Lemon Yellow acrylic paint on the palette paper.

③ Apply the mixed paint to the starfish stamp using the wedge sponge. Stamp starfish in a random manner over the box and lid. Reload the stamp as required. Allow the paint to dry. Wash the stamp and wedge sponge and blot them dry on a paper towel.

④ In a well-ventilated area, spray a coat of matte spray finish to protect the stamped images. Allow the spray to dry, and assemble the box and lid.

⑤ To create the barrette bow, cut 100 5" lengths of light blue Wraphia. Attach the end of the floral wire paddle to one end

of the barrette. Group five pieces of blue Wraphia together at a time. Position the first group at the same end as the wire. Wrap the wire around the center of the grouping. Add the next grouping of five directly against the first. Wrap the wire around the center of the second grouping. Continue this process until all cut lengths have been attached to the barrette. Secure the wire to the

opposite end of the barrette and cut the excess wire using the wire cutters. Clip the dolphin hair clips to the ends of the Wraphia pieces.

⑥ Insert light blue tissue paper into the box to create a soft background for the starfish.

⑦ Wrap the box with the yellow filmy ribbon and tie a shoelace bow. Attach the barrette to the shoelace bow.

⑧ To create the small vellum snap box in the photograph, repeat the same paint and stamp process as above. Wrap the box with yellow filmy ribbon, and attach seashell hair clips down the tails of the bow.

GIFT TAG IDEA

1. For a coordinating gift tag, stamp both the flower and the starfish on a piece of white card stock.
2. Cut the images out, leaving a 1/4" border.
3. Using the punch, make a hole in the top of the tags and attach them to one of the ends of ribbon.

CHALK **IT UP**

Materials:

- ⁜ 1 package soft yellow tissue paper
- ⁜ 1 package purple tissue paper
- ⁜ 2 packages colored chalk
- ⁜ Spool O' Ribbon:
  - 1 roll narrow soft yellow
  - 1 roll narrow soft green
  - 1 roll narrow white
- ⁜ 25' of 1 1/2" filmy lilac ribbon
- ⁜ 2 mini hard-bottom cellophane bags
- ⁜ 1 textured piece of fabric or textured tablecloth
- ⁜ 1 can matte finishing spray

- ⁜ 1 Sharpie Fine Point Black Permanent Marker
- ⁜ 1 Scotch Pop-up Tape Strip Dispenser
- ⁜ 1 roll Scotch Double-Stick Tape
- ⁜ 1 Scotch Permanent Adhesive Glue Stick
- ⁜ silver floral wire

Tools:

- ⁜ Fiskars all-purpose scissors
- ⁜ Fiskars acrylic ruler with two-color grid
- ⁜ wire cutters

Instructions:

① Lay the textured fabric flat on the work surface. Lay the purple sheet of tissue paper flat on top of the fabric.

② Break a 1" piece of green chalk. Starting at the top left-hand corner of the tissue, place the chalk on its side and move the chalk, applying slight pressure, to create a 1" x 1 1/2" square. The chalk will pick up some of the texture from the fabric below. Drop down 1 1/2" and repeat the square. Repeat this process until you reach the bottom of the tissue. Go back to the top of the tissue, drop down 1 1/2" from the first chalked square, and repeat the same process until you reach the bottom of the tissue. One row of squares will be offset to the next, creating a checkerboard effect. Continue this pattern until the sheet of tissue paper is completed.

③ Using the grid ruler and yellow chalk, draw vertical lines down the middle of each row of green squares. Draw horizontal lines through the middle of each row of green squares. Use the grid on the ruler to ensure even and properly spaced lines.

④ In a well-ventilated area, lightly spray the chalked surface of the tissue paper with matte finishing spray to set the chalk. Allow the tissue to dry.

⑤ Wrap the gift, referring to "Gift-Wrapping Basics: How to wrap a tube," and leave the ends open.

⑥ Cut six 12" lengths of each of the three colors of Spool O' Ribbon. Place one length of each color together and tie one end to the package. Repeat this process on the opposite end of the package

⑦ Cut two 6' lengths of filmy ribbon. Make two loopy bows. Refer to "Bow-Making: How to make a loopy bow."

⑧ Attach the bows over the Spool O' Ribbon bows on each end. Trim the excess wire with the wire cutters.

GIFT TAG IDEA

1. Enhance the front bottom of the mini cellophane bag with a square of decorated tissue paper.
2. Use a glue stick to attach the decorated square to the mini cellophane bag.
3. Write your gift tag message on the tissue with a black marker.
4. Insert the chalk into the bag and secure the bag with an 18" piece of each color of narrow ribbon – and tie the ribbons in a shoelace bow. Refer to "Bow-Making: How to make a shoelace bow."
5. Wire a 7" loop of filmy lilac ribbon over the center of the shoelace bow. Trim the excess wire with wire cutters.
6. Cut the ends of the lilac ribbon into an inverted "V" shape. To attach the gift tag, tie one of the ribbons from the box to one of the ribbons on the gift tag.

PACKAGE #2

① Use soft yellow tissue paper to wrap a second package.

② Wrap the lilac ribbon around all sides of the box and tie a knot at the top.

③ Over this knot, tie six 12" lengths of each of the three Spool O' Ribbon colors.

④ Make a florist bow using 9' of lilac ribbon. Refer to "Bow-Making: How to make a florist bow."

⑤ Wire the bow over the center knot at the top of the box and trim the excess wire with the wire cutters.

IT'S JUST A **GAME**

Materials:

+ Giant Snakes & Ladders game with plastic game mat
+ colored Wraphia to match colors of the game
+ 1 roll Scotch Tear-By-Hand Packing Tape

Tools:

+ Fiskars all-purpose scissors

Instructions:

① Lay the plastic game mat right-side down on a flat work surface.

② Place the gift in the middle of the game mat. If the mat is extremely large, you may need to fold it in half, or fold in the ends to make it fit your gift.

③ Wrapping plastic is somewhat different than wrapping with paper. Wrap the plastic game mat around the gift box and draw it together on the underside of the box.

④ Use a piece of the packing tape to hold the plastic game mat in place. Most other tapes will not stick to the plastic, and it's important that the tape be removed without damaging the plastic game mat.

⑤ To wrap the gift, refer to "Gift-Wrapping Basics: How to wrap a box."

⑥ To decorate the package, cut a long strand of each of the four colors of Wraphia. Wrap the four colors of the Wraphia around the back of the box, criss-cross the Wraphia and bring it back to the top of the box. Tie a snug knot.

⑦ Create a large shoelace bow using three long strands of each color of Wraphia and attach it to the gift. Refer to "Bow-Making: How to make a shoelace bow."

⑧ Attach the game-playing pieces to the bow, using single strands of Wraphia.

GIFT TAG IDEA

It's fun to incorporate some of the characters featured in the game on your gift tag. For instance, if you are wrapping with a game that has dots, use small round spouncers (generally used for stenciling) to create dots on the gift tag. If the game has creatures, incorporate those images into a unique and fun card. Remember to have lots of fun along the way. Your gift will be the hit of the party.

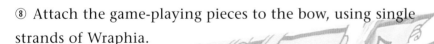

GONE "BUGGY"

Materials:

- 1 large brown bag with handles
- 1 medium brown bag with handles
- 16′ neon-colored Wraphia
- 1 small package black pony beads
- 1 Painter's Opaque Paint Marker, Fine Black
- DecoArt Americana acrylic paints:
  - 1 bottle Bright Green
  - 1 bottle Yellow Light
  - 1 bottle Tangelo Orange
  - 1 bottle Country Red
  - 1 bottle Lamp (Ebony) Black
- tissue paper:
  - 1 package bright yellow
  - 1 package neon green
  - 1 package black
- 2 clear mini cellophane bags
- 1 package assorted plastic bugs
- 1 package 3/4" color-coding labels
- 1 Scotch Pop-up Tape Strip Dispenser
- paper towels
- water container
- large trash bag
- palette paper

Tools:

- Loew-Cornell liner paintbrush
- Loew-Cornell double-ended stylus
- Fiskars all-purpose scissors
- Fiskars circle hand punch

Instructions:

① Cover the work surface area with an opened trash bag.

② Lay the large brown bag out flat.

③ Squeeze a puddle of each of the five acrylic paint colors onto the palette paper.

④ To make ladybugs, dip the pad of your thumb into the puddle of Country Red acrylic paint. Press your thumb down on the bag, making a red imprint. Repeat this process randomly, printing several red thumbprints on the bag. "Reload" your thumb as necessary. Wash and dry your hands.

⑤ Dip your middle finger into the Bright Green paint. Use this finger to make a series of three imprints placed close together. Repeat this process randomly, printing several more images on the bag. Reload your finger as necessary for each imprint. Wash and dry your hands.

⑥ Dip your pinky finger into the puddle of Tangelo Orange acrylic paint. Use this finger to make two imprints opposite each other. Repeat this process randomly, printing several more orange images on the bag. Reload your finger as necessary for each print. Wash and dry your hands.

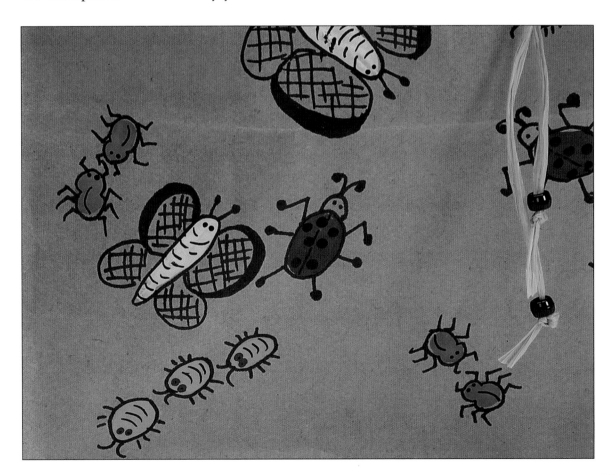

⑦ Dip the side-length of your pinky finger into the Yellow Light acrylic paint. Press the side of your pinky onto the bag, making a long yellow imprint. Repeat the imprint several times randomly on the bag, reloading your finger as necessary.

⑧ Insert the end of the paintbrush into the Country Red acrylic paint. Make two dots for eyes on each of the green bugs. Reload the paintbrush for each dot. Wash the end of the paintbrush and blot it dry on a paper towel.

⑨ Insert the end of the paintbrush into the Lamp (Ebony) Black paint. Make several black dots on the backs of each red ladybug shape. Reload the paintbrush as required. Wash the the paintbrush and blot it dry on a paper towel.

GIFT TAG IDEA

1. Place two or three plastic bugs in a small cellophane bag and attach it to the handle of the bag with several lengths of Wraphia.
2. Attach a black pony bead to the end of each length of Wraphia and trim to different lengths.
3. Use the color-coding labels and black marker to write your message, and stick the labels to the bottom front of the cellophane bag. I think the idea of attaching a visible extra gift to the bag is very appealing to kids.

⑩ Dip the stylus into the Lamp (Ebony) Black acrylic paint. Make two dots for eyes on each orange bug, reloading for each dot. Repeat the same process on the yellow butterfly bodies. Add black centers to the red eyes on the green bugs. Wash the stylus and blot it dry on a paper towel. Allow all paint to dry.

⑪ Using the black marker, outline all bug shapes. Add antennae to all bugs and butterflies. Detail the bugs with interesting feet, lines to their bodies, and wings to the sides of the butterflies, referring to the photo.

⑫ To decorate the top of the bag, use the punch to make several holes evenly spaced along the top of the bag. Cut two 3' lengths of the neon green Wraphia. Use Scotch Tape to secure one end of each length of Wraphia to the inside of the bag. Feed the Wraphia in and out of the holes, starting at opposite ends, until they meet in the center. Punch another hole, if necessary, to allow both ends to meet on the outside of the bag. Tie the Wraphia together in a shoelace bow. Refer to "Bow-Making: How to make a shoelace bow." Attach a pony bead to the end of each length, tying several knots below it to secure the pony beads in place.

⑬ Wrap the gift in three colors of tissue paper, and allow the tissue to spray out of the top of the bag.

⑭ To create a second, smaller bag, repeat the same process as above, sizing the images down to fit the size of the bag.

TRUCKS & **CARS**

Materials:

- 1 large white baker's cake box or box of your choice
- DecoArt Americana acrylic paint:
  - 1 bottle Cadmium Yellow
  - 1 bottle Bright Green
  - 1 bottle Berry Red
- 3 small toy cars (red, yellow, green)
- 16' of 1" crayon satin ribbon
- Spool O' Ribbon:
  - 1 roll narrow red
  - 1 roll narrow green
  - 1 roll narrow yellow
- 1 Plaid Simply Stencils Car
- 1 black ink stamp pad
- 1 can matte finishing spray
- 1 piece bright paper or card stock

- 1 roll Scotch Long-Mask Masking Tape
- 1 roll Scotch Double-Stick Tape
- floral wire
- water container
- paper towels

Tools:

- Loew-Cornell small sponge brush
- Fiskars all-purpose scissors
- Fiskars circle hand punch
- Plaid medium spouncer

Instructions:

① Lay the box flat on the work surface, right-side up.

② Mask a 1" border on the top, front, back, and bottom of the box.

③ Staying within the border, apply two coats of Cadmium Yellow paint to the front and back panels of the box. Allow drying time between coats. Wash the sponge brush and blot it dry on a paper towel.

④ Staying within the border, apply two coats of Bright Green paint to the top of the box. Allow drying time between coats. Wash the sponge brush and blot it dry on a paper towel.

⑤ Paint the bottom of the box, as well as the two side flaps of the box, with two coats of Berry Red paint, allowing drying time between coats. Wash the sponge brush and blot it dry on a paper towel.

⑥ Apply the stencil to the top of the box, using small pieces of masking tape to hold the stencil in place.

⑦ Dip the medium spouncer in the black stamp pad and dab the ink onto the stencil.

⑧ Lift and move the stencil to another location within the masked-off area and stencil another image. Continue this process until you have an all-over pattern on the top of the box. Allow the ink to dry. Wash the spouncer and stencil and blot them dry on a paper towel.

⑨ Run the wheels of a small toy car through the ink pad. Roll the car over the yellow front panel of the box, staying within the masked-off border. Re-ink the car wheels and continue rolling, creating a random pattern. Repeat the same process on the back yellow panel of the box. Allow the ink to dry. Wash the wheels of the car and blot them dry on a paper towel.

⑩ Spray a light coat of the matte finishing spray over the entire box to set the ink. Allow the finish to dry completely.

⑪ Assemble the box.

⑫ Create a medium florist bow using the 1" satin crayon ribbon. Refer to "Bow-Making: How to make a florist bow." Wire the bow securely.

⑬ Create a large loopy bow using all three colors of Spool O' Ribbon. Refer to "Bow-Making: How to make a loopy bow." Wire the loopy bow to the back of the florist bow.

⑭ Create a smaller loopy bow using all three colors of Spool O' Ribbon. Wire the smaller bow to the top of the florist bow.

⑮ Attach the bow to the top of the box using a piece of double-stick tape. Attach the three toy cars to the top of the box using a piece of double-stick tape.

GIFT TAG IDEA

1. Place the stencil on a brightly colored piece of paper or card stock.
2. Stencil a car image on the paper. Allow the ink to dry.
3. Cut the car image out, leaving a border around the image of aproximately 1/4."
4. Flip the gift tag over and write a message on the back.
5. Punch a hole in the upper area of the car and attach the card to the gift using the tails of the loopy bows.

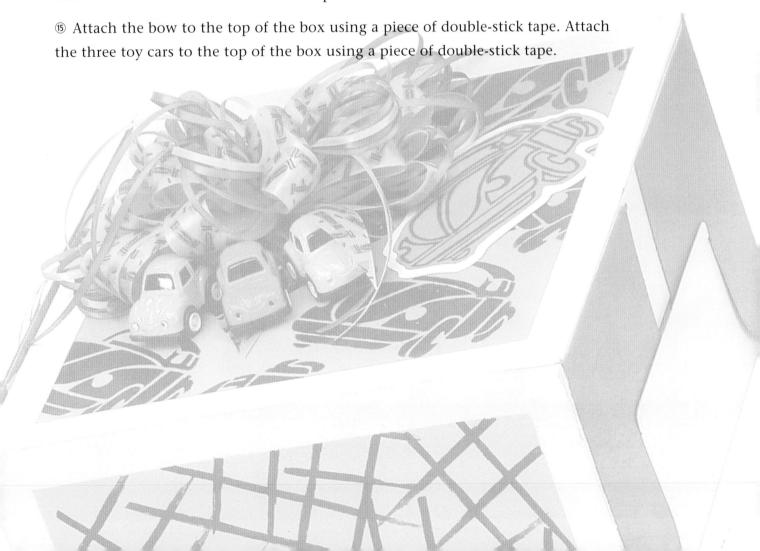

CHAPTER **SIX**

General Occasions

IN THE **JUNGLE**

Materials:

- Rubber Stampede Decorative Stamping African Collection Kit
- 1 bottle DecoArt Dazzling Metallics Bronze acrylic paint
- 1 roll tiger-stripe gift-wrapping paper
- 1 roll narrow black Spool O' Ribbon
- 1 roll 6" copper tulle
- 1 piece black craft paper
- 1 Scotch Pop-up Tape Strip Dispenser
- water container
- paper towels
- disposable latex gloves
- palette paper
- silver floral wire

Tools:

- Fiskars all-purpose scissors
- Fiskars circle hand punch
- small wedge sponge
- measuring tape
- wire cutters
- pencil

Instructions:

① Measure and cut the wrapping paper to fit the gift box. Lay the paper right-side up on the work surface.

② Squeeze a puddle of Bronze acrylic paint onto the palette paper.

③ Choose a decorative tiger stamp or animal stamp of your choice. Use the small wedge sponge to apply Bronze paint to the stamp. Place the stamp in the center of the paper, apply light pressure, and carefully remove the stamp to reveal the image.

④ Reload the stamp with paint and continue applying the images in an all-over design on the wrapping paper. Let the paint dry completely. Wash the stamp and wedge sponge and blot them dry on a paper towel.

⑤ To wrap the box, refer to "Gift-Wrapping Basics: How to wrap a box."

⑥ To create the tulle wrapping, measure around the sides of the box. Cut one length of copper tulle and wrap the tulle around the box, tying a knot at the top.

⑦ To create the tulle bow, cut 12 12" lengths of copper tulle. With all ends of the tulle together, feed the tulle under the knot at the top of the box. Tie the 12 lengths in a knot. Separate the tulle to create a fluffy bow.

⑧ Cut four lengths of black Spool O' Ribbon long enough to tie around the gift. Wrap the ribbon around the box, over the tulle, and tie a knot at the top of the box.

⑨ Measure and cut 16 36" lengths of black Spool O' Ribbon. Gather one end of each length together, and fold the ribbon in half. Wrap a 2" piece of floral wire around the ribbon at the fold and twist the wire to secure. Attach the black ribbon to the underside of the tulle bow. Allow the tails to drape over the box.

PACKAGE #2

① Lay a sheet of white or ivory tissue paper on a flat work surface.

② Use a second animal stamp and silver paint to stamp images on the tissue paper.

③ Finish the design with narrow black ribbon and a bow.

④ Attach little items, like jungle finger puppets or other small items, to enhance the gift.

PACKAGE #3

① Place a sheet of brown tissue paper on a flat work surface.

② Choosing an animal print background stamp, apply black paint onto the stamp.

③ Continue stamping an all-over, cohesive pattern, using the background stamp.

④ Wrap the package with black tulle and finish the top with narrow black curling ribbon.

⑤ Attach a gift tag using the same materials.

GIFT TAG IDEA

1. Apply Bronze paint to a stamp of your choice.
2. Stamp the image onto a piece of black craft paper. Allow the paint to dry.
3. Cut around the stamped image, leaving approximately 1/4" extra around the motif.
4. Punch a hole in the tag, loop a small piece of narrow black Spool O' Ribbon through the hole, and attach the stamped gift tag to the gift.

AROMATHERAPY

Materials:

+ 1 medium-size gift basket
+ 1 small gift basket
+ colored paper:
  • 1 package green
  • 1 package lilac
+ 1 package green self-adhesive paper
+ 1 bottle Victorian rose fragrance oil
+ 1 medium clear spray bottle
+ 1 medium clear lotion bottle
+ 1 bottle unscented hand cream
+ 3 various-sized white square candles
+ 1 mini heart stamp
+ 1 black ink pad
+ 1 bottle white embossing powder
+ Painter's Opaque Paint Markers:
  • 1 Medium Pearlescent Purple
  • 1 Medium White
  • 1 Fine Black
+ 10' of 1 3/4" wired
  lilac ribbon
+ 10' of 1 1/2" filmy
  lilac ribbon
+ 1 roll narrow white
  Spool O' Ribbon
+ 2 white tassels
+ 2 heart-shaped findings
+ 3' of pearls
+ cellophane wrap
+ silver floral wire
+ large trash bag
+ white paper

Tools:

+ Fiskars all-purpose scissors
+ Fiskars acrylic ruler
+ Fiskars paper crimper
+ Fiskars circle hand punch
+ wire cutters
+ embossing heat tool
+ paper shredder

Instructions:

① To make the scented shred, cut 10 sheets of each of the colored papers in half. Run each half-sheet, individually, through the paper crimper. Run each half-sheet through the paper shredder to make brightly colored paper shred.

② To scent the shred, cover the entire work surface area with an open trash bag.

③ Fill the spray bottle with water. Add several drops of Victorian rose oil to the water.

④ Spread the shred on the work surface area and lightly spray with the scented water. Allow the shred to dry. Insert the shred into the large basket.

⑤ To make the spray label, cut a piece of the green adhesive paper to measure 3" wide x 2 1/2" deep. Place the green paper on a sheet of white paper.

⑥ Use the black ink stamp pad and mini heart stamp to apply several hearts along the bottom of the label – and one heart on the top left-hand corner. While the ink is still wet, shake the white embossing powder over the hearts. Lightly shake the excess embossing powder from the label onto the white paper. Return the excess to the bottle for future use. Run the embossing heat tool over the hearts to melt and set the embossing powder.

⑦ Using the white paint marker, write "Victorian Rose Oil" on the top of the label. Create shadows on the lettering with the black paint marker. Remove the backing from the adhesive label and adhere it to the center of the spray bottle.

⑧ To make the Victorian Hand Cream, fill the medium hand-cream bottle with unscented cream. Add several drops of the Victorian rose oil. Mix well.

⑨ Create a similar label for the "Victorian Hand Cream" using the same technique. When completed, center it on the clear lotion bottle.

⑩ To decorate the neck of each bottle, cut a 12" length of the filmy lilac ribbon, tie it in a shoelace bow and attach it to the bottle with wire. Refer to "Bow-Making: How to make a shoelace bow." Include a tassel in the initial knot of each bow.

⑪ Create another shoelace bow for each bottle, using 12" of the

GIFT TAG IDEA

1. Scent the paper in the same manner as the shredded paper.
2. Use the same technique as for the bottles to create a label for the gift tag.
3. Use the punch to create a hole in the corner of the tag and attach it to one of the lengths of ribbon on the gift basket.

white Spool O' Ribbon. Wire the Spool O' Ribbon bow into the middle of the filmy ribbon bow. Glue a heart finding in the middle of the bow. Wire an 18" string of looped pearls around the neck of the bottles.

⑫ To make the heart-decorated candles, heat the surface of the smaller candle using the embossing heat tool. Be careful not to melt the candle too much. While the candle is hot, stamp the mini heart stamp onto the flat front of the candle. Repeat if necessary in the same spot to achieve a visible heart-shape indentation.

⑬ On the longer candles, have a string of hearts down the front of each candle. Color-in the heart indentations using the purple paint marker. Wrap each candle with a piece of filmy lilac ribbon, tied in a shoelace bow.

⑭ Fill the large basket with the spray, hand cream and candles, along with other aromatherapy and bath-type items.

⑮ To wrap the gift basket, lay a large piece of cellophane wrap on a flat working surface. Center the basket on the cellophane. Draw each corner of the cellophane over the handle and up to the middle of the basket snugly. Tie the cellophane with a piece of ribbon and a pretty shoelace bow.

GOLFERS **RULE**

+ 1 plastic luggage tag
+ 1 dark green golf caddy pouch
+ 1 package white 2 1/8" golf tees
+ 1 dark green golf towel
+ 1 container 24 golf balls
+ 1 package dark green golf-club covers
+ 1 package dark green paper crimp
+ 1 package 3 1/2" white diskette labels
+ 1 3" rubber band
+ 1 roll cellophane wrap
+ 1 roll dark green Wraphia
+ palette paper
+ water
+ paper towels
+ disposable latex gloves
+ large trash bag

Tools:
+ Loew-Cornell medium sponge brush
+ Fiskars all-purpose scissors
+ fine-grit sandpaper
+ small screwdriver
+ glue gun and glue sticks
+ computer and color printer

Materials:
+ 1 Walnut Hollow wooden box, with hinged lid
+ DecoArt Americana acrylic paint:
    • 1 bottle Midnite Green
    • 1 bottle Honey Brown
+ 1 can gloss spray finish

Instructions:

① Using the small screwdriver, remove the hinges and separate the top of the box from the bottom. Set the screws and hinges aside.

② Sand the box well and wipe away any dust particles with a damp paper towel.

③ Squeeze a puddle of Midnite Green paint onto the palette paper. Using the sponge brush, apply two coats of green paint to the inside and outside of the bottom of the box. Allow drying time between coats. Wash the sponge brush and blot it dry on a paper towel.

④ Squeeze a puddle of the Honey Brown paint onto the palette paper. Apply two coats of the brown paint to the inside and outside of the top of the box. Allow drying time between coats. Wash the sponge brush and blot it dry on a paper towel.

⑤ Place the two sections of the box on a flat work surface, protected by the large trash bag. In a well-ventilated area, spray two coats of the spray finish to the inside and outside of both sections of the box. Allow drying time between coats.

⑥ To attach the golf-ball feet, turn the bottom of the box upside down. On one corner of the box, measure 1/4" from the two outside edges. Mark the center point with a pencil. Place a dot of glue on the center point and glue one golf ball to the point. Repeat this process on the remaining three corners. Let the glue dry completely.

⑦ To attach the golf-ball "handle" on the front edge of the top of the box, measure to find the center point of the edge of the box. Glue a golf ball to this point. Let the glue dry completely.

⑧ Re-attach the hinges to the box.

⑨ Fill the bottom of the box with green paper crimp.

⑩ Place the remaining golf balls randomly in the shred.

⑪ Insert tees throughout the randomly placed golf balls.

⑫ Fill the golf caddy pouch with the remaining golf tees and set it to one side of the box.

⑬ Fold the golf towel and place in an upright position at the back of the box.

⑭ Measure and cut a piece of cellophane wrap large enough to cover the box, allowing approximately 8" at the top.

⑮ Measure and cut several 36" strands of Wraphia.

⑯ Set the piece of cellophane wrap on a flat work surface. Place the box in the center of the wrap. Gather the wrap from all sides up to the middle point. Tightly wrap the strands of Wraphia around the cello wrap, letting the tails drape down the front.

GIFT TAG IDEA

1. To make the computer-generated gift tag label, open a document, choose the appropriate label setting and set the print font and color of your choice. Type "Golfers Rule!" Place the sheet of labels in the printer and print the label.

2. Remove the cardboard insert from the luggage tag and adhere the printed label to the insert. Reinsert the label into the luggage tag.

3. Feed one end of the elastic band through the handle of the luggage tag. Pull the opposite end of the elastic band up and through. Place the elastic band around the golf-ball handle on the lid of the box, allowing the tag to hang down the inside of the box.

TEACHER'S **PET**

Materials:

- ✢ 1 small wooden basket with handle and lid
- ✢ 1 package teacher-related rub-on images
- ✢ 10' of 1/2" ruler ribbon
- ✢ 1 chalkboard eraser
- ✢ 1 small chalkboard
- ✢ 1 bottle DecoArt Americana Buttermilk acrylic paint
- ✢ 1 bottle DecoArt clear gel stain
- ✢ 1 bottle DecoArt Americana matte varnish
- ✢ 1 bottle Plaid Dimensional White Shiny fabric paint

- ✢ 1 roll narrow black Spool O' Ribbon
- ✢ white tacky glue
- ✢ silver floral wire
- ✢ disposable latex gloves
- ✢ palette paper
- ✢ soft cloth
- ✢ water container
- ✢ paper towels

Tools:

- ✢ Loew-Cornell palette knife
- ✢ Loew-Cornell 1" wash paintbrush
- ✢ Fiskars all-purpose scissors
- ✢ wire cutters

Instructions:

① Mix a ratio of 50% Buttermilk paint with 50% clear gel stain on the palette paper, using the palette knife to blend.

② Use the wash paintbrush to apply this mixture to the entire basket. Remove the excess stain by rubbing into the grain of the wood with the soft cloth. Allow the basket to dry. Wash the paintbrush and blot it dry on a paper towel.

③ Cut apart the various rub-on images. Following manufacturer's directions, rub several of the larger images onto the lid of the basket in a pleasing manner.

④ Rub another image onto the handle of the basket.

⑤ Rub a larger image on the inside of the lid. Put the remaining images aside.

⑥ Using the wash paintbrush, apply two coats of varnish to the entire basket and the inside of the lid. Allow drying time between coats. Wash the paintbrush and blot it dry on a paper towel.

⑦ Cut a piece of ruler ribbon to fit around the front band of the basket. Cut another for the back band of the basket. Squeeze a bead of white tacky glue around the front and back bands of the basket, spreading the glue. Adhere the pre-cut pieces of ribbon to the basket.

⑧ Make a small six-point bow using the ruler ribbon. Refer to "Bow-Making: How to make a six-point bow." Wire the bow securely. With the excess wire, attach the bow to the handle of the basket. Trim the tails of the bow in an inverted "V" shape.

⑨ Tie six 12" lengths of black Spool O' Ribbon around the base of the bow and trim them to different lengths.

TEACHER'S ERASER

① Stain the wooden top of the eraser using the same technique as the basket. When dry, rub one of the saved rub-on images to the top of the eraser.

② Apply two coats of varnish over the rub-on, allowing drying time between coats. Wash the paintbrush and blot it dry on a paper towel.

③ Use the tacky glue to glue a piece of ruler ribbon just up from the edge of the eraser, slightly below the rub-on image.

④ Include this personalized eraser into the teacher's basket, along with other teacher-related items.

GIFT TAG IDEA

1. For the gift tag, personalize a mini chalkboard that can be used to identify the teacher's classroom. Write the teacher's name and the word "Classroom" on the black area of the chalkboard using the white dimensional paint.
2. Treat the wooden exterior frame with the same stain treatment as the basket, allowing the treatment to dry completely.
3. Apply a few remaining rub-on images to the edges of the board, and protect them with two coats of varnish.
4. Attach two 12" lengths of ruler ribbon to the two top outer corners of the chalkboard frame. Once the glue is dry, tie the two pieces of ribbon together in a shoelace bow, creating a hanger for the chalkboard.

GO **FISH**

Materials:

- 1 gift box
- 1 roll white craft paper
- 1 bottle DecoArt Americana Sapphire acrylic paint
- Wraphia:
  - 1 roll blue
  - 1 roll red
  - 1 roll ivory
- 1 small stick
- 1 paper clip
- various-sized fish clip-art images in color (free clip art found at www.FresherImage.com)

- 1 Painter's Opaque Paint Marker, Fine White
- 1 yellow fishnet decoration
- 1 blue fishnet decoration
- 1 roll Scotch Masking Tape
- 1 Scotch Pop-up Tape Strip Dispenser
- 1 Scotch Permanent Adhesive Glue Stick
- water container
- palette paper
- paper towels

Tools:

- Fiskars all-purpose scissors
- toothbrush

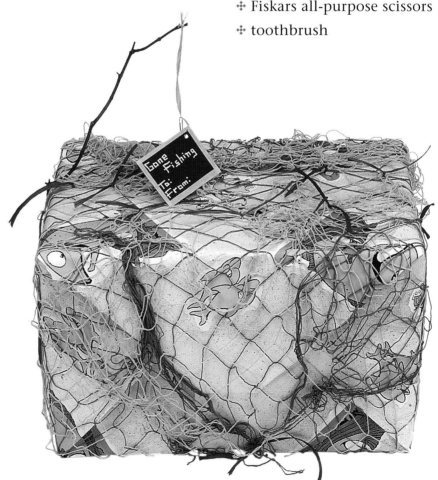

Instructions:

① Measure and cut one piece of white craft paper to fit the gift box. Place the paper flat on the work surface.

② Squeeze a puddle of Sapphire paint on the palette paper. Dip the toothbrush into the water, then into the paint, diluting the paint. Tap off any excess paint on a paper towel.

③ With your finger placed on one end of the toothbrush, run your fingernail down the bristles, splattering the paint across the paper. Repeat this process until the entire sheet of paper is covered with flecks. Let the paint dry completely.

④ Begin tearing around the clip-art images, leaving approximately 1/4" around the edge. Place each image on the paper, moving them around until you are satisfied with the placement.

⑤ Adhere each image to the paper, using the glue stick. Continue this process until all images have been glued to the paper.

⑥ To wrap the gift box, refer to "Gift-Wrapping Basics: How to wrap a box."

⑦ Open the blue fishnet and place it flat on the work surface. Place the gift on top of the net, top-side down.

⑧ Cut six 3" pieces of red Wraphia. Draw the net up each end of the box, feeding one piece of Wraphia at a time through several holes in the net, finishing off with a knot to secure the net in place.

⑨ Repeat the same procedure with the yellow fishnet, securing the net with 3" pieces of blue Wraphia.

GIFT TAG IDEA

1. To make the gift tag, tie a piece of ivory Wraphia to one end of the stick. Tie the other Wraphia end to one end of the paper clip. Open the paper clip to form a hook.
2. Weave the stick through several holes on one side of the fishnet, allowing it to remain upright over the top of the box with the hook visible.
3. Cut a 3" x 5" piece of black craft paper. Create a 1/4" border of masking tape around the black craft paper.
4. Using the white paint marker, write your message on the black craft paper.
5. Punch a hole in one corner of the tag.
6. Feed the extended end of the paper clip through the hole in the tag and stand the tag upright on the top of the box.

GRADUATION

Materials:

+ 1 large red gift bag with handles
+ 1 medium blue gift bag with handles
+ 1 Fiskars School Days – theme decorative stencil
+ 2 graduation specialty papers of your choice
+ 1 sheet black paper
+ 1 package adhesive-backed red holographic film (6" x 8")
+ 1 black permanent marker
+ 1 package red tissue paper
+ 1 package blue tissue
+ 1 package black alphabet and number stickers
+ 1 package polka-dot alphabet stickers
+ 4 sheets white paper
+ Spool O' Ribbon
    • 1 roll narrow red
    • 1 roll narrow blue
+ 1 Scotch Restickable Adhesive Glue Stick

Tools:

+ Fiskars all-purpose scissors
+ Fiskars paper edgers of your choice
+ Fiskars corner edgers of your choice
+ Fiskars stainless steel ruler
+ X-Acto knife
+ pencil

Instructions:

① Center one sheet of the graduation specialty paper on the large red bag. Using the ruler and pencil, measure and mark in 2" from both outside edges of the paper.

② Use the paper edgers to cut the paper along the pencil lines. Trim along the top and bottom edges of the paper.

③ Use the corner edgers to cut a design on the four corners of the paper. Adhere the paper to the center of the red bag using the restickable glue stick.

④ Using the corner edgers, cut the four corners of the red holographic film sheet. Remove the backing, then center and adhere the red film sheet to the graduation specialty paper.

⑤ Cut a piece of white paper that measures 1/2" smaller on all four sides than the red film sheet. Use the corner edgers to trim the corners for a decorative touch.

⑥ Measure, then using the black marker, mark a trim line 1/4" in from the outside edge of the cut white paper. Adhere the white paper to the center of the red film sheet.

⑦ To create the motifs on the bag, position the stencil on black paper and use the pencil to trace one ribbon and two graduation hats. With either the scissors or X-Acto knife, cut out all the motifs.

⑧ Adhere the three components of the ribbon to the center of the white sheet, one graduation hat in the top left-hand corner of the bag, and the other at the bottom right-hand corner.

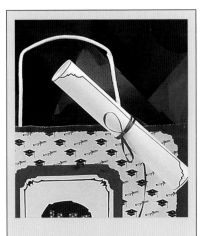

GIFT TAG IDEA

1. To make the certificate gift tag, cut the appropriate size of paper to suit the size of the gift bag.
2. Decorate the corners using the corner edgers.
3. Roll the paper into a scroll with your message included.
4. Tie the scroll with a small piece of ribbon and attach the scroll to one handle of the gift.

⑨ Use the polka-dot stickers to write the graduate's name in the center of the ribbon. Use the black alphabet stickers to write the word "Graduate" down the left-hand side of the bag, below the graduation hat. Write the year of graduation at the top right-hand side of the red bag, above the graduation hat.

⑩ Insert the gift into the bag and fill the top with black and red tissue paper.

PACKAGE #2

① Create a smaller bag using the same instructions, changing the size of the bag to suit a smaller gift.

② Switch the colors to achieve a different look.

BOTTLED **UP**

Materials:

- 1 vellum bottle box
- 1 large hard-bottom cellophane bag
- 1 small hard-bottom cellophane bag
- 1 bottle Plaid Soft Flock, Cobalt Blue
- 13' of 3" royal blue wired ribbon
- 1 roll narrow royal blue
  Spool O' Ribbon
- 1 large package iridescent shred
- 1 Painter's Opaque Paint Marker,
  Fine Black
- white tacky glue
- white card stock
- silver floral wire
- paper towels
- water container
- large trash bag
- palette paper

Tools:

- Fiskars all-purpose scissors
- Fiskars circle hand punch
- wire cutters

Instructions:

① Cover the entire work surface area with an open trash bag. Lay the vellum bottle box flat on the covered work surface.

② Ensure all glue designs stay below the top flap of the box. Using the nozzle of the glue bottle as a guide, draw an exaggerated "S" on the front panel of the box. Repeat several of the "S" shapes in various directions. Fill in the empty areas with simple curl shapes.

③ Trim the tip of the flock fiber bottle 1/8" above the top line. Hold the applicator bottle approximately 3"- 4" away from the wet glue and squeeze the bottle in short bursts. Continue until the glue is covered with the fiber. Allow the glue to dry overnight.

④ Once the glue is dry, shake the excess fiber onto the trash bag. Return the excess to the applicator bottle for future use.

⑤ Assemble the bottle box, insert a bottle and surround the bottle with iridescent shred.

⑥ Cut a 3' length of royal blue wired ribbon. Make a simple shoelace bow with long inverted "V"-cut tails. Refer to "Bow-Making: How to make a shoelace bow."

⑦ Repeat the same process with the royal blue Spool O' Ribbon. Attach the two together using a 12" length of floral wire. Wire the bows to the side of the bottle box. Trim the excess wire with the wire cutters.

PACKAGE #2

① Use the same glue-and-fiber technique on a sheet of white tissue paper. Allow the design to dry thoroughly.

② Cut a piece of cellophane wrap the same length as the tissue, but 12" wider.

③ Center the tissue paper in the middle of the cellophane wrap, decorated-side down.

④ Position the bottle in the center of both papers. Carefully draw the four corners of the tissue paper to the top of the bottle. Tie temporarily around the neck of the bottle with a 3' length of royal blue Spool O' Ribbon. Draw up the four corners of the cellophane wrap and hold it together around the neck of the bottle.

⑤ Remove the ribbon from the tissue paper and tie both papers together around the neck of the bottle.

⑥ Top the bottle off with a royal blue shoelace bow.

GIFT TAG IDEA

1. Using the same technique as above, draw four "S" designs in glue on the card stock. Apply the flock fiber in the same manner as above, allowing the glue to dry and shaking off the excess.
2. Cut around the "S" shapes, leaving a 1/2" border.
3. Punch a hole at the top of the gift tag.
4. Use the back of the gift tag to write your message in black marker.
5. Tie the tag onto one of the lengths of Spool O' Ribbon.

PACKAGE #3

① Draw a white glue "S" design in the middle of the large cellophane bag.

② Apply the flock fiber in the same manner as above, allowing the glue to dry.

③ Shake the excess fiber off and return it to the applicator bottle.

④ Insert a bottle into the bag and surround it with iridescent shred.

⑤ Tie the top of the cellophane bag with a shoelace ribbon bow. This can be repeated using a smaller hard-bottomed cellophane bag.

SWEET PACKAGING

Materials:

- ✢ white gift box of your choice
- ✢ 1 package lime-green wrapped candies
- ✢ 1 package orange wrapped candies
- ✢ 1 roll lime-green curling ribbon
- ✢ 1 roll orange curling ribbon
- ✢ DecoArt Americana acrylic paints:
  - • 1 bottle Olive Green
  - • 1 bottle Tangelo Orange
- ✢ 1 can matte finishing spray
- ✢ card stock
- ✢ 1 Painter's Opaque Paint Marker, Fine Black
- ✢ 1 Scotch Permanent Adhesive Glue Stick
- ✢ paper towels
- ✢ water container
- ✢ palette paper
- ✢ silver floral wire
- ✢ disposable latex gloves
- ✢ large trash bag

Tools:

- ✢ Fiskars all-purpose scissors
- ✢ Fiskars circle hand punch
- ✢ wire cutters
- ✢ toothbrush

Instructions:

① Cover the work surface with an open trash bag. Disassemble the gift box and lay it flat on the covered work surface.

② Squeeze a puddle of each of the two acrylic paint colors on the palette paper (separate puddles).

③ Wearing the latex gloves, dip the toothbrush into the water container and remove the excess water on a paper towel. Dip the toothbrush into the Olive Green paint. Run your index finger across the toothbrush bristles, splattering the paint over the white box surface. Repeat this process, reloading the toothbrush as necessary until you have the desired effect. Wash the toothbrush and remove the excess water on a paper towel.

④ Repeat the same process with the Tangelo Orange paint, creating an all-over splattered look. For variety, there should be some very fine splatters and some very thick ones for a splash of color. Allow all paint to dry thoroughly. Wash the toothbrush and remove the excess water on a paper towel.

⑤ In a well-ventilated area, lightly spray the painted surface of the box with the matte finishing spray. Allow the box to dry. Reassemble it.

⑥ Cut a length of each color of the curling ribbon long enough to wrap around all four sides of the box, criss-crossing the ribbon on the bottom of the box and drawing it back up to the top. Secure the ribbon in a knot on the center-top of the box.

⑦ To create the bow, cut eight 30" lengths of each of the curling ribbon colors. Tie them in a knot, four at a time, over the center knot on the top of the box. Using the scissors, curl the ribbon tails.

⑧ To create the candy flower, attach one end of the wire to the end of one of the lime-green candies. Add a second candy, wrapping the wire around the end, as with the first candy. Continue adding four more candies, for a total of six, securing them together in a bunch. This is the candy flower center. Start adding the orange wrapped candies, one at a time, wiring each one under one of the lime-green candies. Continue this process until eighteen orange candies are surrounding the lime-green flower center. Wrap the wire around the base several times to secure everything in place, and cut the wire with the wire cutters, leaving a 12" length. Wire this length and the candy-flower bow over the center knot on the top of the box. Cut the excess wire.

GIFT TAG IDEA

If the truth be told, I am a huge candy lover. My family can attest to the fact that I have been known to taste-test candy when making these wonderful candy bows, in the name of love. With this in mind, I thought it would be fun to inject a little humor into a coordinating gift tag.

1. Cut a piece of card stock approximately 3" x 4".
2. Use the glue stick to attach a flattened candy wrapper to the front of the card stock.
3. Cut a second piece of card stock, approximately 3" x 2". Use the paint marker to write your message on the rectangle. Glue the rectangle to the candy wrapper on an angle.
4. Cut a starburst shape approximately 3" x 2".
5. Use the paint marker to write the message "Taste tested in the name of friend-ship!"
6. Glue this shape to the bottom of the gift tag, allowing it to extend off the bottom.
7. Punch a hole in the top left-hand corner of the gift tag and attach it to one of the curling ribbon strands.

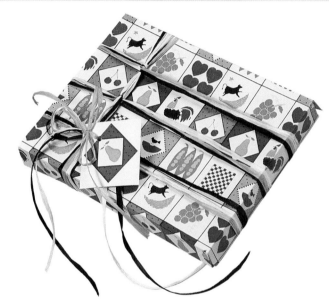

CHAPTER **SEVEN**

Cuisine Wrapped in Style

BASKET **BONANZA**

Materials:

+ 1 medium basket with handles
+ 1 small basket with handles
+ 25' of 2" yellow-and-white
  checked ribbon
+ 2 rolls narrow yellow Spool O' Ribbon
+ 1 medium cellophane bag
+ 1 small cellophane bag
+ 5' - 6' of plaid flannel
+ 1 sheet red self-adhesive paper
+ 1 sheet white paper
+ 1 "From the Kitchen Of" rubber stamp
+ 1 Fiskars rainbow dye ink pad
+ 1 Painter's Opaque Paint Markers:
  • 1 Fine Red
  • 1 Fine Black
+ 1 Scotch Pop-up Tape Strip Dispenser
+ 1 Scotch Permanent Adhesive
  Glue Stick
+ several jars homemade jams, jellies
  and preserves
+ 2 small boxes crackers of
  your choice
+ 2 packages cream cheese of
your choice

+ 6 small cheese knives
+ silver floral wire
+ paper towel

Tools:

+ Fiskars all-purpose scissors
+ Fiskars stainless steel ruler
+ 1 Fiskars heart punch
+ wire cutters

Instructions:

① Using the scissors, cut a square of the plaid fabric to fit inside the medium basket, allowing enough fabric to cover the interior of the basket and fold over all four sides.

② Fringe the edges of the fabric by removing several threads from each side.

③ Insert the fringed fabric square into the basket so each corner is extending over the sides of the basket.

④ Cut a 6" square of plaid fabric to cover each jar top of homemade jam, jelly and preserve. Fringe the edges of all fabric squares.

⑤ Remove the twist tops of all jars. Center a fringed fabric square on a jar top. Carefully replace the twist top over the fabric square. Ensure the top is screwed on tightly. Tie a 24" length of yellow Spool O' Ribbon around the twist top and into a shoelace bow. Refer to "Bow-Making: How to make a shoelace bow." Repeat the same process for each remaining jar top.

⑥ Use the heart punch to create several heart stickers from the red self-adhesive paper. Remove the backing and adhere one heart to the center of each shoelace bow on the jar lids. Add a heart to each of the jar labels.

⑦ Using the yellow-and-white checked ribbon, make a large six-point bow. Refer to "Bow-Making: How to make a six-point bow." Wire three 24" lengths of yellow Spool O' Ribbon to the back of the bow.

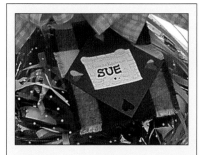

GIFT TAG IDEA

1. Cut a 5" plaid fabric square and fringe the edges.
2. Cut a 3" square of red adhesive paper.
3. Punch a heart in each corner of the square.
4. Remove the backing from the adhesive paper and adhere it kitty-corner to the plaid fabric square.
5. Ink the rubber stamp in the rainbow stamp pad. Position the top half of the stamp in green and the bottom in blue. Test the stamp on a corner of the white paper until you are pleased with the image. Stamp the image onto the white paper. Allow the ink to dry. Wash the rubber stamp and blot it dry on a paper towel.
6. Using the red paint marker, write your name below "From the Kitchen Of."
7. Cut out the stamped image.
8. Use the glue stick to adhere the stamped image to the center of the red adhesive paper square.
9. Using the scissors, remove the fabric from behind the top heart. This will allow you to feed a 24" piece of yellow Spool O' Ribbon through the open heart and attach it in a knot under the bow at the top of the cellophane bag.

⑧ Insert several jars into the basket. Place the basket in the medium cellophane bag. Tape the excess bag at the base around the back of the basket. Tie the top of the bag with the wire from the six-point bow. Trim the excess wire with the wire cutters and the ends of all ribbon tails with scissors.

BASKET #2

This basket is simply a miniature version of the medium basket. If you make home preserves, what a lovely house warming gift. The pepper jelly could be combined with crackers and cream cheese, along with small cheese knives, for a yummy snack presentation. Think about this idea as a great gift for teachers, the bus driver, coaches, neighbors – and don't forget family and friends.

LUXURY **LOAVES**

Materials:

- various loaves of favorite breads
- colorful placemats
- colorful tissue paper
- 10" x 20" printed cellophane bag
- colored Wraphia or string
- mini plastic clothespins
- colorful plastic spring hairclips
- freezer paper
- 2" decorative ribbon to wrap around
- 1 Scotch Pop-up Tape Strip Dispenser

Tools:

- Fiskars all-purpose scissors
- Fiskars circle hand punch

Instructions:

Wrap a regular-sized loaf of freshly baked bread in something that will be useful for the recipient at a later date, like a placemat, tea towel, or large napkin. These items can be used in the bottom of a breadbasket, once the bread is sliced and being served. Be sure to wash, dry and press the fabric item before wrapping the bread.

① To create a fabric bread caddy, lay a placemat, tea towel or napkin face down on a flat working surface.

② Place the loaf of bread in the middle of the placemat.

③ Turn over approximately 1" of one end of the placemat.

④ Draw the placemat up the end of the bread, folding the sides of the placemat up at the same time. Neaten the edges and use the mini plastic clothespins to hold the placemat in place.

⑤ Repeat the same process on the opposite end of the loaf.

⑥ Wrap a piece of 2" ribbon around the center of the loaf and tie a shoelace bow on the top of the bread. Decorate the bow with several mini clothespins. Refer to "Bow-Making: How to make a shoelace bow."

PACKAGE #2

① For smaller loaves, and for loaves that have more fat in them, wrap the bread first in freezer wrap.

② Lay a placemat, tea towel or napkin right-side down on a flat working surface.

③ Wrap the loaf, drawing the placemat up and around the center of the loaf.

④ To finish off the ends, gently roll the remaining placemat on the ends up to the end of the loaf.

⑤ Hold the placemat in place with colorful plastic spring hairclips.

PACKAGE #3

① Italian loaves are a wonderful gift to make, give and receive. This size of loaf can be decorated beautifully.

② Simply wrap the loaf first in colorful tissue paper, then insert the tissue-covered loaf into a printed cellophane bag.

③ Cut the cellophane bag to size.

④ Use Scotch Tape to neatly seal the open end of the bag.

⑤ Tie small pieces of colorful Wraphia, string or ribbon around each corner of the cellophane bag.

GIFT TAG IDEA

When giving a home-made loaf of bread, it's always fun to attach the recipe in the form of a gift tag. Simply fill out a regular recipe card, perhaps one that has a nice motif on it. Punch a hole in the upper right-hand corner of the recipe card, and attach it to the bread, using either ribbon or perhaps a mini clothespin.

GROW A **GIFT**

Materials:

- 4 6" ceramic-lined clay pots
- 4 12" cotton table napkins
- Delta Stencil Magic Stencil – Seed Packets Border
- DecoArt Americana acrylic paint:
  - 1 bottle Pumpkin
  - 1 bottle Crimson Tide
  - 1 bottle Hauser Medium Green
  - 1 bottle Hauser Dark Green
- 1 bottle DecoArt Textile, medium
- 1 roll narrow green Spool O' Ribbon
- 1 Scotch Pop-up Tape Strip Dispenser
- 6' of white curling ribbon
- palette paper
- water container
- paper towels

Tools:

- Loew-Cornell stencil brushes 1/4", 1/2" and 3/4"
- Fiskars circle hand punch
- iron and ironing board

Instructions:

① Bake home-made muffins, breads or loaves of your choice, filling each of the clay pots.

② Wash, dry and press the 12" cotton table napkins, removing any sizing.

③ Squeeze a puddle of each of the paint colors on the palette paper (separate puddles). Using a two-part paint to one-part textile-medium ratio, create fabric paints by blending the medium into each color of paint.

④ Place one napkin on a flat work surface. Place the flower motif of the stencil on the napkin in one corner. Dip the 1/2" stencil brush into the Hauser Dark Green paint, remove any excess paint on a paper towel, and stipple in an up-and-down motion, filling in the flower. Repeat this process on the remaining three corners and around the edges of the napkin in a pleasing manner. Repeat the entire process on the other cotton napkins. Wash the stencil and stencil brush and blot them dry on a paper towel.

⑤ Using the same technique as above, stencil a radish on two of the napkins, and a carrot on two napkins. Let the paint dry completely. Wash the stencil and stencil brush and blot them dry on a paper towel.

⑥ Use the scissors to cut four 12" lengths of green ribbon.

⑦ Place one clay pot upside down on a flat work surface. Center one napkin right-side up, on top of the pot, with the stenciled design at the front of the pot. Fold the sides of the napkin like a package and tie a 12" length of green ribbon around the pot. Repeat this for the other three pots.

⑧ Referring to "Gift-Wrapping Basics: How to make a cellophane gift bag," make four cellophane bags.

⑨ Place the baking into the clay pots and insert the pots into the cello bags.

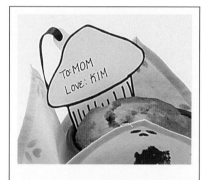

GIFT TAG IDEA

1. To make the muffin gift tag, either use a template or draw the shape of a muffin free-hand on a piece of craft paper.
2. Use the scissors to cut around the muffin shape, leaving a small space at the top for the ribbon.
3. Print your message on the gift tag.
4. Use the punch to make a hole in the space at the top.
5. Cut a 6" length of green ribbon. Feed one end of the ribbon through the hole in the gift tag and tie it around one bag.

LADYBUG'S **PICNIC**

Materials:

- 1 medium-to-large round glass container with metal lid
- Rust-oleum Painter's Touch:
  - 1 can Gray Primer
  - 1 can Apple Red
- 1 package bees and ladybugs rub-on transfers
- 1 package 36 stick-on ladybugs
- 1 set ladybug salt & pepper shakers
- 1 large mosquito net
- 1 white food tent
- 1 package red gingham plastic food covers
- 1 25" x 30" cellophane bag
- Wraphia:
  - 1 roll white
  - 1 roll red
- assorted jars of jam, bean salad, tea biscuits, cookies and other picnic goodies that will fit in the jar
- 1 roll Scotch Long-Mask Masking Tape
- large trash bag
- glass cleaner
- paper towels

Tools:

- Fiskars circle cutter and craft mat
- Fiskars all-purpose scissors
- Fiskars circle hand punch
- computer and printer
- computer labels

Instructions:

① Remove the lid from the glass container. In a well-ventilated area, place the lid on a flat surface protected by the trash bag. Lightly spray one coat of Gray Primer over the top of the lid. Let the primer dry completely.

② Spray the lid with two coats of Apple Red spray paint, allowing drying time between coats. Set the lid aside.

③ Wash the jar with warm soapy water and dry the inside and outside thoroughly with a paper towel. Clean the outside of the container with glass cleaner and paper towel to prepare it for the rub-on design.

④ Remove the backing (from the sheet of rub-on transfers). Following the manufacturer's instructions, rub several motifs along the top ridge of the glass container, front and back.

⑤ Cut and adhere several other motifs from the sheet of transfers to the glass container in a pleasing manner, using the same technique as above.

GIFT TAG IDEA

1. To make the computer-generated gift tag label, open a document on your computer, choose the appropriate label setting and set the print font and font color of your choice. Type in "Ladybug's Picnic." Insert the labels into the printer and print.
2. Set the circular cutter on the printed label and cut around the label to fit the smallest plastic food cover. Remove the label backing and adhere it to the center of the food cover.
3. Use the punch to make a hole close to the edge of the cover. Insert one tie from the bow through the hole and position the label against the bow.
4. Remove the backing from one ladybug and adhere it to the side of the printed label.

⑥ Cut one 36" length of each of the red and white Wraphia. Wrap the two pieces of Wraphia around the top of the container and knot them in the front.

⑦ Remove the rubber stoppers from the ladybug salt & pepper shakers. Fold one white and one red tail of Wraphia in half. Insert the folded Wraphia into one of the shakers. Replace the rubber stopper and allow the ladybug to hang down the front of the container. Repeat this process with the second shaker, allowing it to hang approximately 1/2" lower than the first one.

⑧ Place plastic gingham lid covers on homemade jars of jam, salads, or any other culinary delight that you want in the container. Fill the container with goodies and replace the lid.

⑨ Cut one 36" length of each of the red and white Wraphia. Make a loopy bow. Refer to "Bow-Making: How to make a loopy bow." Attach the bow to the handle of the lid by the tails.

⑩ Remove the backing and attach several of the small ladybug stick-ons randomly to the bow and the bow-tails.

⑪ Fold the mosquito net in an accordion fashion. Tie the middle of the net with two 6" lengths of red and white Wraphia.

⑫ To ready your gift for the recipient, place the container in the center of the cellophane bag, with the mosquito net behind it. Place the remaining plastic lids between the container and the mosquito net. Gather the cello bag at the top and tie with two 25" lengths of red and white Wraphia. Place the food tent in the middle of the Wraphia knot and tie a shoelace bow. Refer to "Bow-Making: How to make a shoelace bow."

IT'S ALL IN **THE DELIVERY**

Materials:

- 2 12" x 14" sheets white cardboard
- 1 roll 3/4" Scotch Printed Tape – Hearts
- Spool O' Ribbon:
  - 1 roll red
  - 1 roll purple
- 1 8" x 11" gift box
- 1 roll self-adhesive drawer-liner
- Wraphia:
  - 1 roll black
  - 1 roll ivory
  - 1 roll white
- 1 9" x 9" x 5" clear plastic box

- 3 large sheets red tissue paper
- 1 bottle satin varnish
- water container
- paper towels
- palette paper

Tools:

- Loew-Cornell 1 1/2" wash paintbrush
- Fiskars all-purpose scissors
- Fiskars acrylic ruler
- Fiskars circle hand punch
- Fiskars plain brayer
- pencil

Instructions:

① To make the box, use the white cardboard and refer to "Gift-Wrapping Basics: How to make a simple box." Set the lid of the box aside.

② Lay the box right-side down on a flat work surface. Fold the flaps of the box to create the sides. Hold two sides of the box together and tape them in place with a piece of Hearts tape. Repeat this step for all four sides of the box to create a cube. Refer to the photograph for further assistance.

③ Decorate the remaining edges of the box with strips of Hearts tape.

④ To finish the box lid, place it flat on the work surface, right-side down. Fold the four edges up. Turn the lid right-side up and begin adhering the flaps of the lid along the folded edge, using the same procedure as the box.

⑤ Measure and cut one 36" length of each of the red and purple curling ribbons. Make a curling ribbon bow. Refer to "Bow-Making: How to make a curling ribbon bow."

PACKAGE #2

① Disassemble the 8" x 11" box and lay it flat on the work surface.

② Lay the adhesive drawer-liner right-side down. Trace the bottom of the box onto the wrong side of the adhesive drawer-liner, allowing an extra 1/4" around the edges.

③ Cut the adhesive drawer-liner along the pencil lines.

④ Lay the bottom of the box flat, right-side up on a flat work surface. Remove the backing of the adhesive drawer-liner. Adhere the drawer-liner to the box and press in place, using a brayer to flatten.

⑤ Fold the 1/4" extra adhesive drawer-liner over all edges of the box and flatten. Reassemble the bottom of the box, using a spot of hot glue to secure the corners.

⑥ Repeat this process with the top of the box. Place the top and bottom together.

⑦ Measure and cut one 72" length of each of the black, white and ivory Wraphia.

GIFT TAG IDEA

1. Use the scissors to cut a heart shape from the remaining cardboard.
2. Hold the Hearts tape dispenser in one hand and the cardboard heart in the other. Edge the heart with the tape, leaving one-half of the tape on one side of the heart, and the remaining edge folded over to the back of the heart. Allow the tape to "ruffle" on the rounded edges.
3. Punch a hole in the top of the card.
4. Cut two 6" lengths of each of the red and purple curling ribbon. Place the two lengths together and feed one end through the hole, pulling until the ends meet.
5. Feed one end under the bow on the top of the package and tie to the ribbon.

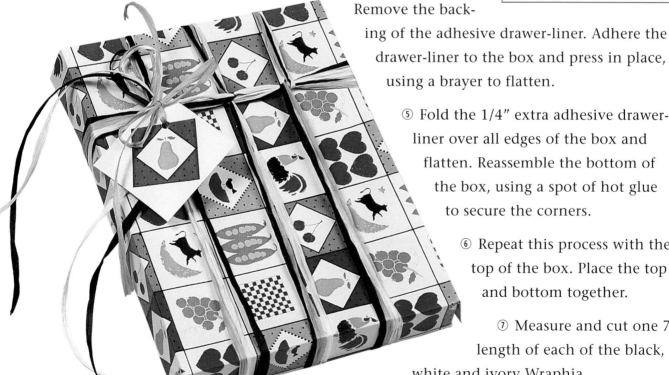

⑧ Place the three lengths of Wraphia on the work surface. Place the box top-side down on the center of the Wraphia. Bring both ends of the Wraphia together and cross, approximately one-quarter of the way down the box. Bring the Wraphia around the sides to the front of the box, and knot. Continue this process, criss-crossing the Wraphia down the box as per the photograph. Finish with a shoelace bow. Refer to "Bow-Making: How to make a shoelace bow." Allow the ends of the Wraphia to drape over the edge of the box.

PACKAGE #3

① Remove the lid from the 9" x 9" x 5" plastic box and set aside.

② Squeeze a puddle of varnish onto the palette paper.

③ Scrunch one piece of red tissue paper into a small ball. Gently spread the tissue out and begin tearing into various-sized pieces. Repeat with the other two sheets of tissue.

④ Load the paintbrush with the varnish and begin applying the varnish to one corner of the lid. Place one piece of the scrunched tissue paper on the varnished area, firmly pressing the paper in place. Repeat this process to cover the entire lid, overlapping the edges for a neat finish. Apply a final coat of varnish, flattening the paper as much as possible. Let the varnish dry completely.

⑤ Repeat this process on the bottom of the box. Let the varnish dry completely. Wash the brush and blot it dry on a paper towel.

⑥ When completely dry, place the lid on the box.

⑦ Cut one 36" length of each of the red and purple curling ribbons. Place the ribbon on the work surface. Place the box upside down on the ribbon. Bring the two ends of the ribbon up and around the box, twist in the center, wrap around the opposite sides and bring to the center of the top. Tie a knot in the center of the box.

⑧ Cut six 36" lengths of each color of ribbon and, holding them together, feed one end under the knot on the top of the box and tie in a knot. Use one edge of the scissors to curl each strand of ribbon.

> ## GIFT TAG IDEA
> 1. Make a gift tag by cutting a 3" square of cardboard.
> 2. Cut a singular motif from the adhesive drawer-liner.
> 3. Remove the backing of the motif and adhere it to the cardboard tag.
> 4. Punch a hole and tie the tag to the package using the bow ends.

MIX IT UP

+ 1 cornmeal muffin recipe to yield
  approximately 10 cups mix
+ 1 package plain recipe cards
+ Painter's Opaque Paint Markers:
    • 1 Green
    • 1 Yellow
    • 1 Brown
    • 1 Black Calligraphy
+ curling ribbon:
    • 1 roll emerald
    • 1 roll white
    • 1 roll yellow
+ 1 1" x 20" cello bag
+ palette paper
+ paper towels
+ glass cleaner
+ water
+ large trash bag

Tools:
+ Loew-Cornell round
  paintbrush
+ Fiskars all-purpose
  scissors
+ Fiskars acrylic ruler
+ Fiskars circle hand
  punch

Materials:
+ 1 medium glass container and
  metal lid with handle
+ 1 wooden spoon
+ Rust-oleum Painter's Touch:
    • 1 can Gray Primer
    • 1 can Sun Yellow
+ Loew-Cornell Accents rub-on
  transfers: hen and rooster
+ 1 rooster utensil holder
+ 1 set rooster tea towels

Instructions:
① Remove the lid from the glass container. In a well-ventilated area, place the lid on a flat surface protected by the trash bag. Lightly spray one coat of Gray Primer over the top of the lid. Let the primer dry completely.

② Spray the lid with two coats of Sun Yellow spray paint, allowing drying time between coats. Set the lid aside.

③ Wash the jar with warm soapy water, and dry the inside and outside thoroughly with a paper towel. Clean the outside of the container with glass cleaner and paper towel to prepare it for the rub-on design.

④ Follow the manufacturer's instructions to adhere a hen motif to the front of the jar. Carefully remove the backing sheet, ensuring all of the transfer has been applied to the glass. If, as you are removing the backing sheet, you find any of the parts of the transfer are not adhering to the glass, replace the sheet and rub over the area again.

⑤ Using the green paint marker, begin making small strokes to resemble grass around the bottom of the container.

⑥ Repeat the same process, using the brown paint marker to accentuate the green grass.

⑦ Using your favorite cornmeal muffin recipe, layer the dry muffin mix in the container.

⑧ Replace the lid on the container.

⑨ Remove one wooden spoon from the rooster utensil holder. Cut three 12" lengths of each of the yellow, green and white curling ribbons.

⑩ Place the spoon under the lid handle. Feed one end of the ribbon under the spoon and around the handle of the container and tie a shoelace bow. Let the ribbon trail down the front of the container.

⑪ To present the gift, place the container, utensil holder, and tea towel set in the center of the cellophane bag. Gather the top and tie it with one 24" length of each of the yellow, green and white curling ribbons.

GIFT TAG IDEA

1. Using a green paint marker and ruler, draw a line around the outside edge of a recipe card.
2. Using a yellow paint marker, draw a second line approximately 1/8" in from the green line.
3. Use the black calligraphy paint marker to write your message to the recipient.
4. Write the recipe for the cornmeal muffins on the back of the recipe card.
5. Use the punch to make a hole in the top left-hand corner of the recipe card. Feed one end of one piece of the trailing curling ribbon through the hole, position the card at the top of the container, and tie the ribbon in a knot.

CHAPTER **EIGHT**

Make It A Memory

PICTURE **PERFECT**

Materials:
- ⊹ 1 gift box
- ⊹ 1 roll red shiny gift wrap
- ⊹ color photocopies of original photos
- ⊹ 2 sheets coordinating memory paper
- ⊹ 1 sheet white card stock
- ⊹ 1 gold certificate label
- ⊹ 1 roll string
- ⊹ Wraphia:
  - 1 roll blue
  - 1 roll yellow
- ⊹ 1 Painter's Opaque
  Paint Marker,
  Fine Black
- ⊹ 1 Scotch Pop-up Tape
  Strip Dispenser
- ⊹ 1 roll Scotch Double-
  Stick Tape
- ⊹ 1 Scotch Permanent
  Adhesive Glue Stick
- ⊹ paper towels

Tools:
- ⊹ Fiskars all-purpose scissors
- ⊹ Fiskars acrylic ruler
- ⊹ Fiskars circle hand punch
- ⊹ Fiskars circle cutter and craft mat
- ⊹ pencil

Instructions:

① Measure and cut the red gift-wrap to fit the box. Allow enough for a crisp fold and to neatly finish the ends of the package. To wrap the box, refer to "Gift-Wrapping Basics: How to wrap a box."

② Cut several images from the color photocopies. Arrange the cut images in an interesting manner on the top surface of the gift.

③ Once you are pleased with the arrangement, begin gluing the images to the gift-wrap, using the glue stick.

④ Cut several images from the first sheet of memory paper. Use the glue stick to adhere the images between the photos.

⑤ Cut several different images from the second sheet of memory paper. Use the glue stick to adhere these images around all four sides of the gift package.

⑥ Use a sheet of paper towel to gently rub over the images, removing any excess glue from the edges.

⑦ Cut enough string, yellow Wraphia and blue Wraphia to wrap around the box on the diagonal. Put the string and Wraphia together and wrap the gift on the diagonal around the bottom end up to the top end of the gift box. Tie a shoelace bow. Refer to "Bow-Making: How to make a shoelace bow." Tie a knot at the end of each tail.

GIFT TAG IDEA

1. Use the circle cutter and craft mat to trace and cut a 3" circle from the white card stock.
2. Center the gold certificate label on the tag.
3. Use the circle cutter to trace and cut a 2" circle from the white card stock.
4. Center and glue the 2" circle on top of the gold label.
5. Use the black paint marker to write a personal message on the gift tag.
6. Glue a few smaller images to the tag.
7. Punch a hole in the tag and attach it to the gift, using the tails of the string and Wraphia.

FRAMED

Materials:

+ 1 gift box
+ 1 roll white wrapping paper
+ 1 sheet white self-adhesive paper
+ several color photocopies of zoo-related original photos, including one large photo
+ 10' of black cording
+ 1 Painter's Opaque Paint Marker, Fine Black
+ 1 package zebra-print tissue paper
+ 1 package Fiskars photo corners
+ 1 package Fiskars photo stickers
+ 1 Scotch Permanent Adhesive Glue Stick
+ 1 Scotch Pop-up Tape Strip Dispenser
+ 1 roll Scotch Double-Stick Tape
+ 1 can 3M Spray Mount
+ paper towels
+ large trash bag

Tools:

+ Fiskars all-purpose scissors
+ Fiskars acrylic ruler with two-color grid
+ Fiskars oval cutter and self-healing mat
+ Fiskars circle hand punch
+ X-Acto knife
+ glue gun and glue sticks
+ pencil
+ eraser

Instructions:

① Measure and cut the white gift-wrap to fit the gift box. Allow enough for a crisp fold and to neatly finish the ends of the package. To wrap the gift, refer to "Gift-Wrapping Basics: How to wrap a box."

② In a well-ventilated area, on a flat surface covered with the trash bag, spray a light coat of the spray mount onto the top surface of the white self-adhesive paper. Lay a sheet of the zebra tissue paper, right-side up, on the tacky surface. Smooth the tissue paper gently in place. Use the X-Acto knife to trim the excess tissue paper. This creates the mat.

GIFT TAG IDEA

1. Punch a hole in the oval cut from the mat.
2. Write your message on the decorative side of the oval gift tag using the black paint marker.
3. Attach the oval to one of the shoelace cording bows.

③ Place the mat on the craft mat. Position the oval cutter to a 4" cutting measurement. Using the ruler, find the center point of the mat. Place the oval cutter on that point. Grasp the knob and rotate the oval cutter in the direction of the arrow on the blade carriage. The finished cut will be 4" in width and 5" in length. Remove the oval shape from the center to use as a gift tag. The backing sheet should still be in place.

④ Lay the mat face down. Remove the backing sheet. Center and adhere the large photo face down on the mat.

⑤ Using the scissors or the X-Acto knife, cut various zoo animals from the color copies. Adhere the photos to the front of the mat in a pleasing manner. Feather leaves with the scissors to create some dimension. (Refer to photo.)

⑥ Using the glue gun, adhere 3' of the black cording around the exterior of the oval-shaped main photograph. Tie the loose ends in a knot at the bottom.

⑦ Place four to six photo stickers on the back of the mat.

⑧ Place a photo corner on each corner of the mat.

⑨ Center the mat on the gift package and adhere it in place.

⑩ Cut the remaining black cording in two. Wrap the first piece around one end of the box and tie a shoelace bow on the top. Refer to "Bow-Making: How to make a shoelace bow." Repeat the same process with the second piece of cording. Knot the ends to avoid fraying. This mat is easily removed from the package and framed at a later date.

VINTAGE **MONTAGE**

Materials:

- ⊹ 1 12" X 9" vellum snap box with lid
- ⊹ black-and-white photocopies of original family pictures
- ⊹ 5' of 1/2" wide black trim
- ⊹ 5' of 2" white filmy ribbon
- ⊹ 1 pewter heart finding
- ⊹ 2 pewter flower findings
- ⊹ 2 sheets black, acid-free paper
- ⊹ 1 Painter's Metallic Paint Marker, Silver Calligraphy
- ⊹ 1 bottle satin varnish
- ⊹ 1 Scotch Permanent Adhesive Glue Stick
- ⊹ water container
- ⊹ paper towels

Tools:

- ⊹ Loew-Cornell 1" wash paintbrush
- ⊹ Fiskars micro-tip scissors
- ⊹ Fiskars acrylic ruler
- ⊹ Fiskars self-healing mat with grid
- ⊹ X-Acto knife
- ⊹ glue gun and glue sticks
- ⊹ needle and white thread

Instructions:

① Choose enough black-and-white photocopied pictures to cover the top surface of the lid of the box.

② Cut around the chosen images, creating an interesting shape using the micro scissors or X-Acto knife.

③ Use the glue stick to adhere four to six of the images to the black, acid-free paper. Cut around the black paper, allowing a 1/4" border around the images.

④ Position the images on the box lid, piecing the photos like a puzzle. Place the images (adhered to the black paper front) and center on the box. Some pictures will tuck under and others over. Play with the images until you are pleased with the results and they cover the entire lid of the box.

⑤ Using the glue stick, adhere the pictures to the box lid.

⑥ Apply two coats of varnish over the top of the box lid using the wash paintbrush. Allow drying time between coats. Wash the paintbrush and blot it dry on a paper towel.

⑦ With the glue gun, adhere the black trim around the exterior of the box lid.

⑧ Wrap the filmy white ribbon around the box on the diagonal. Tie the ribbon in a shoelace bow and sew the heart finding to the center of the bow. Refer to "Bow-Making: How to make a shoelace bow." Cut the two tails in an inverted "V". Sew the two flower findings to each of the tails.

GIFT TAG IDEA

1. Choose a favorite photo-copied picture and cut it into an interesting shape.
2. Adhere it to black paper and cut around it, once again leaving 1/4" border or shadow around the picture.
3. Use the silver paint marker to write "My Memories" on the black border of the tag.
4. Rim the exterior of the gift tag in silver by drawing the silver paint marker around the outside edge of the black backing paper.
5. Adhere the tag to the base of the heart finding.

DESTINATION **HIGH SKY!**

Materials:

- ✤ 1 large white gift bag with handles
- ✤ color photocopies of plane or vacation-related pictures
- ✤ 1 Plaid jumbo vehicles stencil
- ✤ 1 bottle DecoArt Americana Indian Turquoise acrylic paint
- ✤ 1 Painter's Opaque Paint Marker, Black Calligraphy
- ✤ 1 large sheet white paper

- ✤ 1 package black tissue paper
- ✤ 1 blue plastic luggage tag
- ✤ 6' of 4" white acetate ribbon
- ✤ 10" of white fabric trim
- ✤ 1 Scotch Permanent Adhesive Glue Stick
- ✤ latex disposable gloves
- ✤ water container
- ✤ paper towels
- ✤ large trash bag

Tools:

- ✤ Fiskars micro-tip scissors
- ✤ Fiskars acrylic ruler
- ✤ pencil
- ✤ eraser
- ✤ sea sponge

Instructions:

① Cover the entire work surface area with the trash bag.

② Lay the white bag flat on the covered work area.

③ Wearing the latex gloves, dampen the sea sponge with water and squeeze any excess onto a paper towel.

④ Dip the damp sea sponge into the Indian Turquoise acrylic paint. Remove the excess paint on a paper towel. Randomly sponge the front surface of the bag. While the paint is still wet, flip the sponge over and swipe across the paint with the clean damp side of the sponge at an upward angle. This technique creates what appears to be fast-moving sky. Allow the paint to dry.

⑤ Repeat the same technique on all remaining white areas of the bag, allowing all paint to dry completely. Wash the sea sponge and blot it dry on a paper towel.

⑥ Punch out the plane image from the jumbo plane stencil. Place the plane image on the white paper. Trace around the plane using the pencil. Measure and add 1/2" border around the entire plane. Cut the image out.

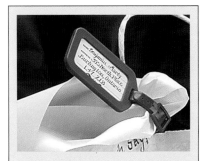

GIFT TAG IDEA

1. To finish the look, create the aviator scarf and gift tag. Cut and glue a 4" piece of fabric trim to the edge of each end of the acetate ribbon.
2. Gently fold the ribbon in half.
3. Insert the middle of the ribbon through the blue plastic luggage tag.
4. Attach the luggage tag as a gift tag to coordinate with the gift's theme.

⑦ Trace and cut the photocopies of pictures to fit within the inner plane shape.

⑧ Use the glue stick to permanently adhere the pictures to the white traced plane. Erase any pencil lines.

⑨ Create a 1/4" black border around the exterior of the plane using the black paint marker.

⑩ Use the glue stick to glue the plane in the center of the front of the bag, tilting it so the plane appears to be ascending.

⑪ Place the ruler on an angle across the top left-hand side of the front of the bag.

⑫ Using the black paint marker, write and repeat your chosen message across the bag. Continue this process down the front of the bag, allowing approximately 2" - 3" between lines.

⑬ Wrap the gift in black tissue paper, insert the gift into the bag, and insert several sheets of black tissue floating out of the top of the bag.

CHAPTER **NINE**

Christmas Creations

A SPRAY OF **SPARKLE**

Materials:

- ✢ 1 roll bright blue foil wrapping paper
- ✢ 1 roll silver foil wrapping paper
- ✢ 2 sheets bright blue tissue paper
- ✢ 1 roll metallic blue curling ribbon
- ✢ 1 roll metallic silver curling ribbon
- ✢ 1 roll 3" metallic silver wired ribbon
- ✢ 1 can Rust-oleum Painter's Touch, Silver Metallic
- ✢ 1 can matte finishing spray
- ✢ 12 flat snowflake ornaments or flat ornaments of your choice
- ✢ 1 Painter's Opaque Paint Marker, Fine Black

- ✢ several blue and silver metallic fountain bows (purchased)
- ✢ several small colored ornaments
- ✢ 1 Scotch Pop-up Tape Strip Dispenser
- ✢ 1 roll Scotch Long-Mask Masking Tape
- ✢ floral wire

Tools:

- ✢ Fiskars all-purpose scissors
- ✢ wire cutters

Instructions:

① Cut a piece of blue foil to fit the gift box.

② Place the foil face up on the work surface.

③ Adhere strips of masking tape in a vertical fashion down the foil wrapping paper, leaving approximately 1" between each piece.

④ In a well-ventilated area, spray the entire surface of the blue foil paper with the Silver Metallic spray paint until the paper is completely covered. Once the paint is dry, remove the tape to reveal a blue and silver metallic striped paper. Coat the paper with a light spray of the matte finishing spray. Allow the finish to dry.

⑤ Wrap the box in accordance with the instructions in "Gift-Wrapping Basics: How to wrap a box."

⑥ Tie the top of the box with both the silver and blue metallic curling ribbons, allowing long tails to drape down the front of the box. Attach a metallic fountain bow, and three small ornaments.

> ## GIFT TAG IDEA
> Use the snowflake as a gift tag for any of these gift-wrapping ideas. Simply write your message directly on the ornament you have used as decoration. The recipient of your gift will be able to place the ornament on their Christmas tree or use it to decorate during the holiday season.

PACKAGE #2

① Cut a piece of blue foil to fit the gift box.

② Place the foil face up on the work surface.

③ Tear off a piece of tape from the tape strip dispenser. Place the tape in the middle of the foil paper. Continue tearing strips of tape and adhering them to the paper, working out from the middle piece of tape in a starburst pattern.

④ In a well-ventilated area, spray the entire surface of the blue foil paper with the Silver Metallic spray paint until the paper is completely covered. Once the paint is dry, remove the tape to reveal a silver paper with a blue starburst pattern. Coat the paper with a light coat of matte finishing spray. Allow the finish to dry.

⑤ Make a curling ribbon bow for the top of the box. Refer to "Bow-Making: How to make a curling ribbon bow." Top the curling ribbon bow with a blue metallic fountain bow.

⑥ Attach two or three small ornaments to the bow.

PACKAGE #3

① Lay one sheet of blue tissue paper on a flat working surface.

② Place the flat snowflake ornaments in a random pattern on the blue tissue paper.

③ In a well-ventilated area, spray silver just over where the ornaments are placed. Lift the ornaments to reveal a snowflake pattern. Allow the spray paint to dry.

④ Coat the tissue with a light coat of matte finishing spray. Allow the finishing spray to dry.

⑤ Line the decorated tissue with a second sheet of the same colored tissue.

⑥ Wrap the box in accordance with the instructions in "Gift-Wrapping Basics: How to wrap a box."

⑦ Finish the package with a metallic curling ribbon bow and a snowflake ornament.

PACKAGE #4

① Wrap the gift box in silver foil wrapping paper. Refer to instructions in "Gift-Wrapping Basics: How to wrap a box."

② To create the bow, cut 10 12" lengths of 3" metallic wired ribbon. Cut an inverted "V" at both ends of each length.

③ Cut five 36" lengths of the silver curling ribbon.

④ Wrap the 3" wired silver ribbon around the gift, crossing the ribbon over on the bottom of the box and bringing it up to the top of the box. Tie a knot.

⑤ Tie one 12" length of ribbon around the center knot on the top of the box in a vertical fashion. Tie a second 12" length around the center knot in a horizontal fashion. Repeat this process until all 12" lengths have been tied. Separate the petals of ribbon to form a flower.

⑥ Tie the curling ribbon around the base of the flower and curl.

⑦ Insert a blue fountain bow in the center of the flower.

GLORIOUS **GOLD**

Materials:

+ 1 roll gold foil gift wrap
+ 1 roll silver foil gift wrap
+ 1 roll silver foil gift wrap with
    open stars
+ 1 package blue tissue paper
+ 1 roll silver metallic curling ribbon
+ 12" - 15" narrow silver wired ribbon
+ 1 Christmas message stamp
+ 1 roll silver wired ribbon with stars
+ 1 black ink stamp pad
+ 1 bottle fine gold glitter
+ 1 package Loew-Cornell compressed
    sponge
+ 1 bottle DecoArt
    Americana Glorious
    Gold acrylic paint
+ 1 small jar silver
    embossing powder
+ 1 Scotch Pop-up Tape
    Strip Dispenser
+ 1 Scotch Permanent
    Adhesive Glue Stick
+ white tacky glue
+ 1 Painter's Opaque
    Paint Marker,
    Fine Black
+ paper towels
+ white paper
+ silver floral wire

Tools:

+ Fiskars all-purpose scissors
+ Fiskars acrylic ruler
+ Fiskars self-healing mat
+ Fiskars circle hand punch
+ 1 Fiskars Celestial
    3-in-1 corner punch
+ X-Acto knife
+ embossing heat tool
+ pen
+ wire cutters

Instructions:

① Measure and cut the gold foil gift-wrap to fit the gift box. Allow enough for a crisp fold and to neatly finish the ends of the package. To wrap the gift, refer to "Gift-Wrapping Basics: How to wrap a box."

② On the cutting mat, use the X-Acto knife and ruler to cut a 6" x 6" square of silver foil paper. These dimensions may need to be adjusted to match the size of your gift box.

③ Use the glue stick to adhere the silver foil square to the center front of the wrapped gift box.

④ Cut a 5" x 5" square of gold foil gift-wrap.

Carefully tear the edges to produce a square that is approximately 4" x 4".

⑤ Adhere the torn gold foil square to the center of the silver foil square.

⑥ Place the Christmas stamp on the black stamp pad and ensure the stamp is well inked. Test the image on a piece of paper. Reload the stamp and press the stamp on the center of the torn gold square. Lift the stamp to reveal the image. Allow the ink to dry overnight. Wash the stamp with soap and water and blot it dry on a paper towel. Decorate the box with ornaments or decorations of your choice.

PACKAGE #2 (silver package)

① Measure and cut the star silver foil gift-wrap to fit the gift box. Allow enough for a crisp fold and to neatly finish the ends of the package.

② Lay the silver foil flat on the work surface, right-side up.

③ Use the pen to draw a simple star, approximately 1" x 1" on the compressed sponge. Cut the star out, place it in water and allow it to expand. Remove any excess water with a paper towel.

④ Squeeze a puddle of Glorious Gold paint on the palette paper. Load the star sponge with the gold paint. Remove the excess paint on a piece of paper towel. Sponge gold stars in between the large white stars on the gift-wrap. Reload the star sponge as necessary. Allow the paint to dry completely. Wash the sponge and blot it dry on a paper towel.

⑤ Fill the centers of the open white stars with the white tacky glue.

⑥ While the glue is still wet, cover the stars with glitter. Allow the glue to dry overnight. Shake the excess glitter off the paper and onto a sheet of white paper. Create a funnel and return the excess glitter to the bottle.

⑦ To wrap the gift, refer to "Gift-Wrapping Basics: How to wrap a box."

⑧ Wrap the box with the silver wired ribbon, criss-crossing the ribbon on the bottom of the box and drawing it back to the top. Tie the two ends of the ribbon together in a double knot at the top front of the box. Cut off the excess ribbon.

⑨ With the remaining ribbon, make a florist bow. Refer to "Bow-Making: How to make a florist bow." Wire the bow over the double knot on the front of the package.

GIFT TAG IDEA

1. To make a coordinating gift tag, cut one open star from the star wrapping paper.
2. Use the glue stick to adhere one cutout to a piece of white paper.
3. Cut the star out again, leaving a 1" border to increase the size of the gift tag.
4. Use the punch to make a hole at the top of one of the star's points.
5. Attach the gift tag to one of the ribbon tails from the bow. Alternatively, try personalizing the actual gift by writing a message directly on the gift, using the black paint marker.

PACKAGE #3 (small gold package)

① Using a slow-drying pigment ink pad, a jar of silver embossing powder and an embossing heat tool, stamp the gold foil wrap with randomly placed Christmas-tree images.

② Cover them with embossing powder and shake off the excess powder. Return it to the jar.

③ Emboss the stamped trees with the embossing heat tool.

④ Finish off with decorations of your choice.

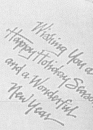

CANVAS **CREATIONS**

Materials:

✤ 2 canvas wine bottle bags with handles, approximately 16" x 8"

✤ Delta Stencil Magic Stencils:
- Christmas Sayings
- Snowman Medley
- Noel Monogram Magic
- Ornament Spray

✤ DecoArt Americana acrylic paint:
- 1 bottle Midnite Blue
- 1 bottle Titanium White
- 1 bottle Lamp (Ebony) Black
- 1 bottle Country Red
- 1 bottle Tangelo Orange
- 1 bottle Yellow Ochre
- 1 bottle Pineapple
- 1 bottle Light Cinnamon
- 1 bottle Hauser Dark Green
- 1 bottle Hauser Light Green

✤ 1 sheet heavy-weight canvas color card stock

✤ 10' of blue wired ribbon

✤ 10' of green plaid ribbon

✤ 1 can 3M Spray Mount

✤ 1 roll Scotch Long-Mask Masking Tape

✤ paper towels

✤ water container

✤ palette paper

✤ silver floral wire

Tools:

✤ Fiskars all-purpose scissors

✤ Fiskars acrylic ruler

✤ Fiskars circle hand punch

✤ 4 Loew-Cornell 1/8" stencil brushes

✤ wire cutters

Instructions:

① In a well-ventilated area, spray the back of all stencils with the spray mount.

② Center the Christmas Sayings stencil, incorporating the word "Joy" at the top of the canvas wine bag.

③ Squeeze separate puddles of all acrylic paints (except the greens), on the palette paper. Use one brush per two colors, cleaning between colors if necessary.

④ Load a stencil brush with the Midnite Blue paint. Remove the excess paint on a paper towel. Stencil the word "Joy" on the bag, working in a circular motion.

⑤ Load a stencil brush with the Titanium White paint. Remove the excess paint on a paper towel. Stencil the small snowman to the right of the word "Joy."

⑥ Load a stencil brush with the Lamp (Ebony) Black paint. Remove the excess paint on a paper towel. Stencil the top hat on the snowman. With little paint left on the stencil brush, create shadows on the snowman by stenciling around the exterior of the three snowballs that create the snowman.

⑦ Load a stencil brush with the Light Cinnamon paint. Remove the excess paint on a paper towel. Stencil the stick arms of the snowman.

⑧ Center the "Snowman Medley" stencil approximately 1" up from the bottom of the bag. With the same stencil brush, stencil the broomstick Light Cinnamon.

⑨ Load a stencil brush with the Yellow Ochre paint and stencil the broom.

⑩ Load a stencil brush with the Pineapple paint. Remove the excess paint on a paper towel. Create highlights over the Yellow Ochre.

⑪ Using the stencil brush previously used for the black paint, reload the brush, remove the excess paint on a paper towel, and stencil the snowman's eyes, mouth, buttons, mitts, and boots.

⑫ Load a stencil brush with the Tangelo Orange paint. Remove the excess paint on a paper towel. Stencil the carrot nose.

⑬ Load a stencil brush with the Country Red paint. Remove the excess paint on a paper towel. Stencil the entire sweater and band.

⑭ Using the stencil brush previously used for the Midnite Blue paint, reload the brush, remove the excess paint on a paper towel, and stencil the scarf and checkered base of the snowman. With little paint remaining in the stencil brush, shade over the Country Red on the interior of the sweater.

⑮ Using the stencil brush previously used for the white paint, reload the brush, remove the excess on a paper towel, and randomly stencil snowflakes surrounding the "Joy" message and the two snowmen.

⑯ Shade the snowflakes with the little paint left on the Midnite Blue stencil brush. Wash all stencil brushes and stencils. Blot them dry on a paper towel.

⑰ Make a six-point bow using the blue wired ribbon, wire it together and attach it to one side of the front handle of the bag. Refer to "Bow-Making: How to make a six-point bow."

PACKAGE #2

① Position the "Noel" stencil approximately 1" down from the top of the bag.

② Stencil the word "Noel" using the Hauser Dark Green paint. Remove the stencil, wash it and blot it dry on a paper towel.

③ Position the greenery and bow from the "Ornament Spray" stencil in the center of the wine bag.

④ Stencil the bow Country Red and the greenery Hauser Dark Green. Add highlights to the greenery with the Hauser Light Green and shadows with the Country Red. Wash the stencil and brushes and blot them dry on a paper towel.

⑤ Make a six-point bow using the green plaid ribbon. Refer to "Bow-Making: How to make a six-point bow." Wire it together. Attach the bow to one side of the front handle of the wine bag.

HOLIDAY **TOOLS**

Materials:

✢ 1 wooden caddy with handle
✢ 1 Plaid stencil – Merry Christmas
✢ Plaid Soft Flock:
- 1 bottle Christmas Red
- 1 bottle Hunter Green

✢ Plaid Fun-to-Paint Fun Sponges, 3 Stars
✢ 1 bottle Plaid Dimensional White Shiny fabric paint
✢ DecoArt Americana acrylic paint:
- 1 bottle Titanium White
- 1 bottle Forest Green
- 1 bottle Calico Red
- 1 bottle satin finish varnish

✢ 10' of 1 1/2" wired plaid ribbon
✢ 1 Painter's Opaque Paint Marker, Fine Black
✢ 1 roll Scotch Long-Mask Masking Tape
✢ silver floral wire
✢ water container
✢ paper towels
✢ palette paper

Tools:

✢ Loew-Cornell 3/4" wash paintbrush
✢ Loew-Cornell foam brush set
✢ Loew-Cornell 1/2" stencil brush
✢ Loew-Cornell palette knife
✢ Fiskars all-purpose scissors
✢ Fiskars circle hand punch
✢ fine-grit sandpaper
✢ wire cutters

Instructions:

① Sand the caddy thoroughly and wipe away any dust particles with a damp paper towel.

② Apply two coats of Forest Green paint using the wash paintbrush to the inside bottom, two sides, two ends, and two side ledges. Allow drying time between each coat. Wash the paintbrush and blot it dry a on a paper towel.

③ Apply two to three coats of Calico Red paint to the handle, allowing drying time between each coat. Wash the paintbrush and blot it dry on a paper towel.

④ Paint the rest of the caddy with two to three coats of Titanium White. Allow drying time between coats. Wash the paintbrush and blot it dry on a paper towel.

⑤ Using the foam paintbrush, apply a coat of the Calico Red paint to the small star sponge.

⑥ Leaving an area for the "Merry Christmas" stencil, apply several small red stars to one area of the exterior of the caddy. Leaving room to apply green stars, continue this process, referring to the photo for placement. Wash the sponges and foam paintbrush and blot them dry on a paper towel.

⑦ Repeat the same process using the Forest Green paint. Allow all paint to dry completely. Wash the sponges and foam paintbrush and blot them dry on a paper towel.

⑧ Outline the stars with the black paint marker.

⑨ Using the foam paintbrush, apply two to three coats of varnish to all areas of the caddy. Allow drying time between coats. Wash the paintbrush and blot it dry on a paper towel.

⑩ Place two pieces of paper under the caddy to catch the excess fiber. Using a damp flat paintbrush, apply a generous coat of Hunter Green Soft Flock adhesive to the inside bottom of the caddy. Immediately apply the flock fiber to the adhesive by squeezing a generous amount from the bottle in short bursts. Allow the fiber to sit for a minimum of one hour before removing the excess onto the paper. Fold the paper and funnel the excess fiber back into the bottle. Repeat this process on the two inside ends of the caddy. Wash the paintbrush and blot it dry on a paper towel.

⑪ To stencil the "Merry Christmas" on the front of the caddy, place the stencil where desired and use a small amount of masking tape to hold the stencil in place. Using the stencil brush, stipple the adhesive onto the stencil message. Work quickly, leaving the stencil in place, and apply the Christmas Red flock fiber. Remove the stencil gently. Allow the fiber to sit for a minimum of one hour and remove the excess flock fiber as above. Wash the stencil brush and stencil and blot them dry on a paper towel.

⑫ Apply a generous coat of white fabric paint onto appropriate areas of the caddy using the palette knife. Stipple the dimensional paint with the flat side of the palette knife, to resemble the texture of snow. Allow the dimensional paint to dry overnight. Wash the palette knife and blot it dry on a paper towel.

⑬ Make a six-point bow using the plaid ribbon. Refer to "Bow-Making: How to make a six-point bow."

GIFT TAG IDEA

1. To create a simple gift tag, cut a piece of card stock, or glue two pieces of paper together.
2. Stamp a star shape onto the paper and allow the paint to dry.
3. Outline the star using the black paint marker.
4. Cut the star out, leaving a 1/8" border around the black outline.
5. Punch a hole at the top of the star and attach it to the caddy using narrow ribbon.

METAL & **MESH**

Materials:

✤ 1 roll Paragal ArtEmboss Metal –
   medium-weight aluminum
   (includes 1 fine-point stylus)
✤ 1 Delta Stencil Magic Stencil –
   Snowman Medley or stencil
   of choice
✤ 1 roll 6" white tulle with silver glitz
✤ 1 roll narrow silver wired ribbon
✤ 1 roll shiny black wrapping paper
✤ 1 Scotch Pop-up Tape Strip Dispenser
✤ 1 Painter's Opaque Paint Marker,
   Fine Black
✤ paper towels

Tools:

✤ Fiskars all-purpose scissors
✤ Fiskars circle hand punch

Instructions:

① Create a pad to work on by layering four sheets of paper towel.

② Place a metal sheet on the pad. Place the "Snowman Medley" stencil on the metal.

③ Trace one ribbon-and-mitten design, using the fine-point stylus and following the manufacturer's instructions. Punch a hole in the top of the design. This will create a gift tag.

④ Trace seven small mitten designs to decorate the bow.

⑤ Trace the large snowman for the side of the gift, referring to the photograph for placement.

⑥ To emboss the designs, flip the metal over and retrace around the design lines several times.

⑦ If using a different stencil, simply follow the same directions to obtain the items desired to decorate the package and create one gift tag.

⑧ Using scissors, trim around the exterior of all designs.

⑨ Wrap the gift with black wrapping paper, referring to "Gift-Wrapping Basics: How to wrap a box." Wrap the gift with tulle and tie the tulle in a knot on the top of the box.

⑩ To create the tulle bow, cut eight to 10 lengths of tulle. Pass one length under the knot on the top of the box and tie another knot. Repeat this process with the other lengths of tulle, tying each one off. Fluff the tulle to create a bow.

⑪ Cut eight 24" lengths of narrow silver wired ribbon. Tie the eight 24" lengths of wired ribbon under the tulle bow. Wrap each ribbon tail around the stylus to create curls.

⑫ Loop one length of curled wired ribbon through the hole punched in the gift tag. Attach the gift tag to the top of the package, in the middle of the tulle bow.

GIFT TAG IDEA

1. Follow the original instructions for tracing and embossing the metal designs.
2. Punch a hole at the top of the design.
3. Using the scissors, trim around the exterior of the tag.
4. Cut a 4" length of narrow wired ribbon, insert one end of the ribbon through the top hole and tie a knot. Curl each end of the ribbon.
5. Use the fine black paint marker to write your holiday message.
6. Attach the gift tag to the gift.

⑬ Punch holes in each of the seven mittens and attach the mittens to the ends of the narrow silver wired ribbon.

PACKAGE #2

① If using the "Snowman Medley" stencil, follow the directions above to trace and emboss the large snowman head on a sheet of metal.

② Trace and emboss an assortment of eight large and eight small mittens.

③ Using the scissors, trim around the designs. If using a different stencil, trace and emboss one large motif for the gift tag, and small motifs to decorate the gift.

④ Using the punch, make a hole in the head of the snowman.

⑤ Create a tulle bow, as above, with curled narrow silver wired ribbon.

⑥ Using double-stick tape, adhere the mittens all over the box to decorate.

ORNAMENTAL

Materials:

+ 1 roll brown craft paper
+ 2 Christmas picks with frosted pinecones and berries
+ 1 small cardboard jewelry box
+ 1 3" grapevine wreath
+ 1 3" plain pinecone
+ 1 package natural raffia
+ 3' of 4" burgundy tartan ribbon
+ 1 roll 1" burgundy tartan ribbon
+ 1 roll narrow gold metallic ribbon
+ 1 roll narrow burgundy Spool O' Ribbon
+ 1 jar DecoArt Outdoor Snow
+ 1 Scotch Pop-up Tape Strip Dispenser
+ 1 Scotch Permanent Adhesive Glue Stick
+ card stock
+ paper towels

Tools:

+ Loew-Cornell palette knife
+ Fiskars circle hand punch
+ glue gun and glue sticks
+ wire cutters

Instructions:

① Make a large brown craft-paper gift bag with raffia handles. Refer to "Gift-Wrapping Basics: How to make a paper gift bag."

② Use the scissors to cut several 36" lengths of raffia and make a shoelace bow. Refer to "Bow-Making: How to make a shoelace bow."

③ Glue the shoelace bow on the top of one side of the bag, between the two handles.

④ To make the grapevine wreath ornament, use the wire cutters to cut two small pieces of greenery from one Christmas pick. Glue the greenery to the top of the 3" grapevine wreath. Make a small florist bow with the burgundy tartan ribbon. Refer to "Bow-Making: How to make a florist bow." Glue the bow between the two pieces of greenery. Add a few small berries from the pick in and around the bow.

⑤ Attach the ornament to the middle of the raffia shoelace bow.

PACKAGE #2

① Wrap the gift in brown craft paper, referring to "Gift-Wrapping Basics: How to wrap a simple box."

② Cut a length of narrow tartan ribbon and wrap the ribbon around the box, criss-crossing the ribbon on the bottom of the box, bringing it back to the top, and securing the ribbon ends with a piece of Scotch Tape.

③ To make the center decoration, cut a 24" length of narrow tartan ribbon and make a small florist bow. Glue two pieces of greenery to the back of the bow. Make a small shoelace bow from raffia. Glue the raffia bow to the center of the florist's bow. Glue a frosted pinecone and two berries to the decoration. Glue the entire bow to the center of the box.

④ To make the ornament, wrap the bottom and lid of a small jewelry box separately, using the 4" wide tartan ribbon, the glue stick and the glue gun. Tie the box with narrow burgundy ribbon. Attach the box to the center ornament, using a small piece of gold ribbon.

GIFT TAG IDEA

1. Cut a piece of card stock large enough to fold in half.
2. Using a glue stick, adhere a piece of ribbon to the front of the card.
3. Decorate the card with a small shoelace bow glued to the upper left-hand corner.
4. Punch a hole in the card and attach it to the gift, using a gold stretch loop or small piece of ribbon.

PACKAGE #3

① Assemble a small green gable box.

② To create the ornament, use the palette knife to apply small amounts of outdoor snow to the bottom and tips of the 3" pinecone. Let the snow dry completely.

③ Use the wire cutters to cut two pieces of greenery from a Christmas pick and glue the greenery to the base of the pinecone.

④ Cut an 8" piece of narrow tartan ribbon and make a shoelace bow. Glue the bow to the center of the greenery on the pinecone.

⑤ Make a small raffia shoelace bow. Glue the raffia bow to the center of the burgundy bow.

⑥ Cut a 12" length of the narrow tartan ribbon and glue the ribbon to the base of the pinecone.

⑦ Wrap and tie both ends of the ribbon through the handle of the box, letting the pinecone ornament drape down the top and front of the box.

FABULOUS **FLORALS**

Materials:

+ 1 roll brown craft paper
+ 1 roll shiny red wrapping paper
+ Spool O' Ribbon:
  - 1 roll narrow green
  - 1 roll narrow red
+ 2 Christmas picks
+ 1 6" grapevine wreath
+ 1 17 1/2" x 9" gift box with removable lid
+ 1 Scotch Pop-up Tape Strip Dispenser
+ 1 roll Scotch Double-Stick Tape
+ 1 Scotch Permanent Adhesive Glue Stick
+ silver floral wire

Tools:

+ Fiskars all-purpose scissors
+ Fiskars paper crimper
+ Fiskars stainless steel ruler
+ Fiskars circle hand punch
+ glue gun and glue sticks
+ pencil
+ wire cutters
+ needle-nose pliers

Instructions:

① Measure and cut the red wrapping paper to fit the bottom of the gift box. Allow enough to neatly finish the ends of the package and fold over the top edge of the box approximately 3".

② To wrap the bottom of the box, lay the red wrap on the work surface, right-side down. Place the box in the middle of the paper. Beginning on one long side, bring the paper to the top edge of the box and fold over. Secure the paper with Scotch Tape. Repeat this process on the opposite side.

③ To finish the ends of the box, fold one side of the paper in toward the center of one end of the box and secure the paper with Scotch Tape. Repeat this process on the opposite side. Draw the center triangle up toward the top of the box and secure it in place with a piece of double-stick Scotch Tape. Repeat this process on the opposite end of the box.

④ Measure and cut the brown craft paper to fit the lid of the box. Allow enough to neatly finish the ends and fold over the bottom edge of the lid approximately 2". Repeat the above process to wrap the lid of the box.

⑤ Measure and cut two 30" x 1 1/2" strips, one 24" x 1" strip, two 12" x 1" strips, and one 4" x 4" square of red wrapping paper.

⑥ Feed all pieces through the paper crimper, one at a time.

⑦ Lay one 30" strip, right-side down, on the work surface. Cover the strip with glue, using the glue stick. Lay the strip diagonally across the top of the box lid from one corner to the opposite corner and gently press to adhere. Repeat this process with the second 30" strip and apply it in the same manner, approximately 3 1/2" from the first strip.

⑧ Use the glue gun to apply a small drop of glue to one end of the 24" x 1" strip and adhere it to the back of the grapevine wreath. Begin wrapping the wreath with the strip of red wrapping paper, allowing parts of the grapevine to show through. Apply another small dot of glue to the end of the paper and adhere it to the wreath.

⑨ Insert and glue one Christmas pick into the wreath.

⑩ Cut one 36" length of each of the green and red Spool O' Ribbon. Make one loopy bow with each ribbon length and wire each bow with a small piece of floral wire. Leave tails on each bow of approximately 12". Refer to "Bow-Making: How to make a loopy bow."

⑪ Using the glue gun, insert and glue each bow into the Christmas pick. Allow the bow tails to trail over the top of the box.

⑫ Cut one 36" x 1" length, one 24" x 3/4" length and one 2 1/2" square of craft paper. Feed each piece through the crimper, one at a time.

⑬ Make a six-point bow with the 36" x 1" strip of crimped craft paper and secure the center of the bow with a piece of Scotch Tape. Refer to "Bow-Making: How to make a six-point bow."

⑭ Use the glue gun to adhere the bow into the bottom portion of the Christmas pick.

⑮ Apply a small dot of glue to each of the 12" x 1" strips of red paper, and adhere them under the tails of the six-point bow.

⑯ Adhere the wreath to the top of the box using four small dots of glue, placing the decorative part of the wreath at approximately "10 o'clock" on the box.

⑰ Use the glue stick to apply glue to the back of the ends of all paper tails and glue them to the box in a pleasing manner.

GIFT TAG IDEA

1. To make the gift tag, use the glue stick to apply a small amount of glue to the back of the 2 1/2" square of craft paper, and adhere it to the middle of the 4" x 4" square of red paper.
2. Make a small loopy bow with the 24" x 3/4" strip of craft paper and adhere it to the bottom corner of the brown square.
3. Using the wire cutters, cut a piece of greenery and ornament from the second pick. Use the glue gun to insert and glue each piece to the bow.
4. Cut one 6" length of each of the red and green Spool O' Ribbon.
5. Use the punch to make a hole in the top corner of the brown square. Feed the two 6" lengths of ribbon through the hole and around the bottom of the wreath and tie them in a bow.

JUST FOR **KIDS**

Materials:

‡ 3 recycled cans with lids, small, medium, large

‡ 1 Delta Stencil Magic Stencil – Mini Gifts Under the Tree

‡ 1 large package assorted neon pompoms

‡ 1 package Velcro dots with adhesive backs

‡ Plaid Dimensional fabric paint:
  • 1 bottle Yellow
  • 1 bottle Green

‡ Embroidery floss:
  • 1 skein yellow
  • 1 skein green
  • 1 skein pink
  • 1 skein orange

‡ Felt squares:
  • 1 neon yellow
  • 1 neon green
  • 1 neon orange
  • 1 neon pink
  • 1 dark green
  • 1 white
  • 6 black

‡ 1 roll narrow yellow Spool O' Ribbon

‡ 1 package star jewels

‡ assorted neon photocopy paper

‡ 1 Scotch Permanent Adhesive Glue Stick

Tools:

‡ Fiskars all-purpose scissors

‡ Fiskars acrylic ruler

‡ Fiskars paper crimper

‡ glue gun and glue sticks

‡ embroidery needle

‡ paper shredder

‡ pen

Instructions:

① Place the large can lengthwise on one piece of black felt. Wrap and fit the felt around the can, trimming all edges with the scissors.

② Glue the felt to the can using the glue stick. Repeat this process with a second piece of black felt to completely cover the can, making sure the edges are flush.

③ Place the lid on another piece of black felt, tracing around the outside edge with the pen. Cut the felt to size. Apply glue to one side of the felt and adhere it to the lid of the can.

④ Repeat the same process to cover the other two cans.

⑤ Place the Mini Gifts Under the Tree stencil on a piece of white felt. Use the pen to trace the star from the top of the tree onto the felt. Remove the stencil and trace around the same star 1/4" from the original edge. Use the scissors to cut the star. Using the star as a template, trace and cut 21 more stars from white felt.

⑥ Decorate the stars using yellow dimensional paint. Allow the paint to dry completely.

⑦ Use the glue stick to adhere one star jewel to the center of each star. Set the stars aside.

⑧ To make the little gifts, cut many different-sized squares of neon pink, neon yellow, neon orange, and neon green-colored felt. Cut smaller-sized squares of felt and glue the smaller pieces onto the larger pieces. Vary the size and colors of the little gifts, keeping them around 1"- 1 1/2" in total size. Braid the different colors of embroidery thread and make small shoelace bows. Refer to "Bow-Making: How to make a shoelace bow." Use the glue gun to glue the bows to the tops of the gifts. Decorate some of the gifts with pom-poms. Make enough gifts to go around the entire bottom edge of the three cans.

⑨ To make two Christmas trees, fold the dark green felt in four. Trace the Christmas tree from the stencil onto the top layer of felt. Cut around the shape of the tree through the four layers.

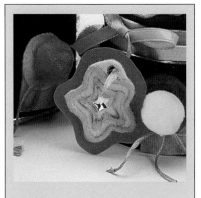

GIFT TAG IDEA

1. Using a pencil, outline any shape on a piece of neon photocopy paper, approximately 5" x 2". Use the scissors to cut out the shape.
2. Place the shape on a piece of white felt and outline the design. Cut the felt shape 1/4" smaller than the template shape.
3. Make three stars as above, apply glue to the back of the three stars and apply them to the felt shape.
4. Apply glue to the back of the felt shape and adhere it to the orange shape.
5. Use the punch to make a hole in one end of the design.
6. Feed one end of the bow on the lid through the tag and tie a knot.

⑩ Thread one 12" piece of yellow embroidery floss through the embroidery needle and tie a small knot in the end. Beginning at one bottom corner of the tree base, stitch around the tree using a blanket stitch. To do a blanket stitch, push the needle up through the two layers of felt, move the needle along slightly, then push the needle back down through the felt, looping the needle through the embroidery thread and gently pulling. Continue in this manner, leaving a 2" opening for the stuffing. Repeat this process for the second tree.

⑪ Stuff the trees with pompom. Finish stitching the opening of each of the trees.

⑫ Use the green dimensional paint to create a zigzag pattern on the trees. Set the trees aside to dry thoroughly.

⑬ Adhere nine of the stars to the top portion and lid of the large can. Repeat this process with the other two cans, distributing the remaining stars evenly.

⑭ Adhere one Velcro dot to the back of each Christmas tree and attach them to the opposite sides of the large can.

⑮ Adhere the gift packages around the base of each of the three cans, distributing them evenly.

⑯ Measure the diameter of each of the can lids and cut a length of yellow Spool O' Ribbon to wrap around each lid, allowing an extra 6" to create a bow and tails.

⑰ Apply glue around the edge of the lids. Adhere the yellow ribbon, allowing enough at each end for a bow. Tie the remaining ribbon in a shoelace bow on each of the cans.

⑱ Create colored paper shred by cutting the neon paper in half, running one piece at a time through the paper crimper, and feeding the crimped sheets through the paper shredder. Alternatively, paper shred is easy to purchase. Fill the cans with colored shred.

CANDY CANE **KEEPERS**

Materials:

- 1 2-quart Chinese food take-out box
- 1 pint Chinese food take-out box
- 1 half-pint Chinese food take-out box
- 1 package holiday-themed tissue paper
- 1 roll cellophane wrap
- Spool O' Ribbon, picot edge
  - 1 roll narrow red
  - 1 roll narrow white
- 1 can 3M Spray Mount
- Painter's Opaque Paint Markers,
  - Fine Red
  - Fine Green
- 1 bag each white and red shred

- white card stock
- silver floral wire

Tools:

- Fiskars all-purpose scissors
- Fiskars stainless steel ruler
- Fiskars self-healing mat
- Fiskars plain brayer
- Fiskars paper crimper
- X-Acto knife
- black pen
- wire cutters
- needle-nose pliers
- paper shredder

Instructions:

① Open the 2-quart Chinese food take-out box and remove the metal handle using the needle-nose pliers. Lay the box flat, right-side up.

② In a well-ventilated area, spray the exterior of the box with spray mount.

③ Position and smooth a piece of the themed tissue paper (right-side up) on the sprayed box. Use the brayer over the entire box to smooth the paper in place.

④ Place the box, right-side up, on the cutting mat. Trim the excess tissue paper from the exterior edges using the X-Acto knife and metal ruler. Open the top slit and holes required to reinsert the metal handle. Go over the box again with the brayer.

⑤ Assemble the box and reattach the metal handle.

⑥ Make a loopy bow using both colors of the Spool O' Ribbon, and wire it to the top of the metal handle. Refer to "Bow-Making: How to make a loopy bow."

⑦ To create shred, cut the sheets of red and white paper in half lengthwise, feed the sheets through the paper crimper, one at a time, and feed several sheets at a time through the paper shredder. Mix the two colors of shred together and use as a filler in the box.

⑧ Fill the box with an assortment of Christmas candy.

GIFT TAG IDEAS

1. Trace a large candy cane onto a piece of card stock.
2. Repeat the process above to adhere a piece of the themed tissue paper to the enlarged candy cane.
3. Use the brayer to smooth the tissue in place.
4. Cut around the candy cane and draw lines around the edges of the motif, using red and green markers.
5. Hook the candy cane around the handles of the large box.

PACKAGES #2 & #3

These Candy Cane Keepers are so fast and simple to prepare, why not make a set of them for gift giving? Follow the same instructions as used for the 2-quart Chinese food take-out box to make the pint and half-pint boxes.

LIGHT IT UP

Materials:

✢ 1 roll white craft paper
✢ 1 roll clear cellophane wrap
✢ 6' of 3" white ribbon
✢ Spool O'Ribbon, picot edge:
  • 2 rolls red
  • 2 rolls blue
  • 2 rolls yellow
  • 2 rolls green
✢ 2 packages of 5 large Christmas light bulbs (1 yellow, 1 red, 1 blue, 1 green, 1 white)
✢ Painter's Opaque Paint Markers:
  • 1 Yellow
  • 1 Red
  • 1 Blue
  • 1 Green
  • 1 Orange
  • 1 Black
✢ 1 mini 6" PVC wreath
✢ 1 3" Styrofoam disc, 1" in depth
✢ 1 6" PVC wreath
✢ 1 Christmas roller stamp (we used "String of Light Bulbs")
✢ 1 green ink stamp pad
✢ 2 packages mini light bulbs
✢ 2 5" sprigs artificial or real pine

✢ white card stock
✢ 1 Scotch Pop-up Tape Strip Dispenser
✢ 1 Scotch Permanent Adhesive Glue Stick
✢ paper towels
✢ silver floral wire

Tools:

✢ Fiskars all-purpose scissors
✢ Fiskars circle hand punch
✢ pencil
✢ glue gun and glue sticks
✢ wire cutters

Instructions:

① Measure and cut the white craft paper to fit the gift box. Allow enough for a crisp fold and to neatly finish the ends of the package.

② Use the pencil to draw a simple Christmas light bulb, to use as a tracer, on the white card stock. Cut the tracer out.

③ Place the white craft paper on a flat work surface, right-side up. Use the tracer and the various colored markers to draw a random pattern of Christmas light bulbs all over the paper.

④ Using the same coordinating color of marker for each light bulb, outline the bulbs well.

⑤ Draw straight lines around the light bulbs to indicate bright light. Draw and color in a "paint splat" shape at the base of each of the light bulbs (refer to the photograph for placement). Draw vertical or horizontal lines along each of the bases. Allow the paint markers to dry.

⑥ Cover the top of the paper with a sheet of cellophane wrap the same size. Treat the two papers as one when wrapping the gift.

⑦ To wrap the gift, refer to "Gift-Wrapping Basics: How to wrap a box."

⑧ Wrap the wide white ribbon around the box on all four sides and finish by tying a knot on the top middle area of the box. Trim away the excess ribbon.

⑨ Repeat the same process using the five Spool O' Ribbon colors, and position them on top of the wide white ribbon for a rainbow effect.

⑩ Using the glue gun, attach the Styrofoam disc to the inside of the PVC wreath. Push and glue the light bulbs into the center of the disc, starting with the white.

⑪ Cut one PVC stem from the wreath and use it to surround the center white Christmas bulb, covering the Styrofoam base. Bring several PVC stems up from the wreath to cover the remaining exposed Styrofoam.

⑫ Make a loopy bow pick by cutting an 8" length of each of the five Spool O' Ribbon colors. Fold them in half as one. Attach a piece of wire 2" down from the fold. Trim the excess wire. Repeat this process five times for a total of six loopy bow picks. Glue a pick to the outside of each of the six Christmas light bulbs.

⑬ Glue a loop of ribbon to the back side of the Styrofoam disc. Use this ribbon to tie the wreath to the center knot at the top of the box.

PACKAGE #2

① To create the round package, measure and cut a piece of white craft paper to fit the package. Allow enough for a crisp fold and to neatly finish the round ends of the package.

② Load the roller stamp on the green ink stamp pad. Roll horizontal lines on the paper, reloading the stamp as required, until the entire paper is covered.

③ Randomly fill in some of the bulb images with the five colored markers.

④ To wrap the gift, refer to "Gift-Wrapping Basics: How to wrap a tube," covering the decorated paper with a sheet of cellophane wrap, as above.

⑤ Cut lengths of all five colors of narrow ribbon and tie a shoelace bow on each of the ends of the gift. Refer to "Bow-Making: How to make a shoelace bow."

GIFT TAG IDEA

On this particular package, make a gift tag by decorating the Christmas light bulb tracer as you decorated the bulbs on the gift-wrap. To give it a different look, outline all of the painted areas with a black permanent marker. Use the back side for your message.

⑥ Tie a mini light bulb decoration to each of the tails of ribbon.

⑦ For a decorative touch, glue the sprigs of pine to the tied sides of the gift.

CHAPTER **TEN**

The Three R's
Reduce – Reuse – Recycle

COMIC **RELIEF**

+ black and red tissue paper
+ brightly colored photocopy paper
+ 1 small bottle Plaid Mod Podge Gloss
+ 1 roll butcher string or twine
+ 1 Painter's Opaque Paint Marker, Medium Black
+ 1 Scotch Permanent Adhesive Glue Stick
+ 1 Scotch Pop-up Tape Strip Dispenser
+ palette paper
+ paper towels
+ water container
+ large trash bag

Tools:
+ Loew-Cornell 1/2" wash paintbrush
+ Fiskars all-purpose scissors
+ Fiskars circle hand punch
+ Fiskars acrylic ruler
+ pencil

Materials:
+ gift boxes, sizes of your choice
+ color comics, either newspaper or comic books

Instructions:
① Cover the work surface with the opened trash bag.

② To wrap the small black box, cover the lid and base of the box separately with black tissue paper, using the glue stick to hold the tissue in place. Refer to "Gift-Wrapping Basics: How to wrap a box."

③ Cut a large single comic from a comic source of your choice to fit the top of the box, less 1/4". Squeeze a small amount of Mod Podge onto the palette paper.

④ Using the paintbrush, apply a layer of Mod Podge to the top of the box. Place and smooth the comic in place, leaving a 1/4" border of black tissue showing. Apply a coat of Mod Podge to the entire outside of the lid. Set the lid aside to dry.

⑤ Measure down, from the top of the box, the width of the lip of the lid. Mark with a pencil.

⑥ Cut enough smaller images to surround the sides and cover the bottom of the base of the box. Using the same process as above, begin applying the smaller comic images, starting from the pencil mark and working toward the bottom of the base.

⑦ Once all comics have been adhered, coat the outside of the base of the box with another coat of Mod Podge. Set aside to dry. Wash the paintbrush and blot it dry on a paper towel.

⑧ When the base and lid are completely dry, tie a piece of string or twine around the outside lip of the lid of the box.

PACKAGE #2 (red box)

① For another great look, wrap a box in red tissue paper.

② Cut four separate comic images, perhaps a theme or series of comics. You may want to choose the recipient's favorite comic strip.

③ Use a glue stick to adhere the comic images in a pleasing manner on the top of the box.

PACKAGE #3 (comic-wrapped box)

① Recycling at its best – simply wrap your gift box in comics taken from a comic book, or the color comics in the newspaper.

② To finish the gift, tie the box with string or twine. Nothing is easier, more inexpensive or better for the environment!

GIFT TAG IDEA

1. Cut a piece of photocopy paper approximately 5" x 7".
2. Fold the paper in half once, and in half again, to create a small folded card.
3. Cut letters from a comic book to create a word image on the card, such as "Laugh" or "Fun."
4. Using the glue stick, adhere the letters or message to the front of the gift card.
5. Use a medium black paint marker to outline the message.
6. Punch a hole in the upper left-hand corner and attach the card to the gift using a small piece of string or twine.

KITCHEN **CAPERS**

Materials:

✢ 1 gift box, any size

✢ 1 roll freezer paper

✢ 1 roll waxed paper

✢ recycled gift wrap

✢ 1 bottle DecoArt Americana,
    Colonial Green acrylic paint

✢ 1 Plaid Stamp
    Décor leaf stamp

✢ 1 roll coordinating 1 1/2" teal ribbon

✢ 1 roll teal curling ribbon

✢ 1 roll lilac filmy ribbon

✢ small place cards

✢ Painter's Opaque Paint Markers,
    various colors

    ✢ 1 Scotch Pop-up Tape Strip
        Dispenser

    ✢ 1 Scotch Permanent
        Adhesive Glue Stick

✢ water container

✢ palette paper

✢ paper towels

Tools:

✢ Fiskars all-purpose scissors

✢ paint roller

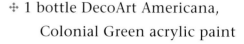

Instructions:

① Measure and cut one piece of white freezer paper to fit the gift box. Place the paper flat on the work surface.

② Squeeze a puddle of Colonial Green paint on the palette paper. Roll the paint roller through the paint, and remove any excess paint on a paper towel.

③ Gently roll the paint roller over the leaf stamp, covering the stamp completely.

④ Starting in the middle of the freezer paper, apply the stamp to the paper, using gentle pressure to ensure that the stamp prints clearly. Remove the stamp to reveal the image. Repeat this process over the entire sheet of paper until you are satisfied with the final result. Allow the paint to dry completely. Wash the paint roller and stamp and blot them dry on a paper towel.

⑤ Wrap the gift box in accordance with the instructions "Gift-Wrapping Basics: How to wrap a box."

⑥ Cut a piece of waxed paper to fit the gift box. Rewrap the box as above, with the waxed paper. The image of the leaf will show through the waxed paper.

⑦ Wrap the gift with a single piece of 1 1/2" teal ribbon. Secure the ribbon in place with tape.

⑧ To create the waxed-paper bow, cut a piece of waxed paper approximately 5" in width and 12" in length. Starting at one end, fold the waxed paper in 1" intervals, going back and forth in a fan fashion.

⑨ Cut a 16' piece of teal curling ribbon. Fold it in half, then half again, and half again. Tie the curling ribbon tight around the middle of the waxed paper fan. Tie a shoelace bow leaving long tails. Refer to "Bow-Making: How to make a shoelace bow." Attach the waxed-paper bow to the center of the 1 1/2" teal ribbon using Scotch Tape.

GIFT TAG IDEA

Using other items for gift tags is not only inventive, but lots of fun.
1. Purchase small place cards, perhaps ones that have a small border, or some other decorative feature. Using paint pens, color in the border, or create a design on the face of the card.
2. Cut small images from the wrapping paper and découpage the images onto the face of the card, using a glue stick.
3. Use the inside of the card for your message.

PACKAGE #2

I love the filmy look that waxed paper gives to a gift. If you're like me, and you save some of the lovely wrapping paper you have received over the years, here's a great way to recycle that same paper.

① Wrap your gift using a pretty piece of previously used wrapping paper.

② Wrap the gift again in waxed paper.

③ Tie a lovely piece of filmy ribbon around the gift.

④ To create the waxed-paper bow, cut eight 12" x 3" pieces of waxed paper. Find the middle of the first piece and hold that piece between your thumb and index finger. Do the same with the second piece, placing it under the first piece, slightly to one side. Continue this process until you have all eight pieces held firmly in the middle. Wrap a small piece of filmy ribbon around the center of the pieces of paper and tie it securely. Move the pieces of waxed paper around to form a flower. Attach the flower bow to the top of the gift with Scotch Tape.

KRAFTY **WRAP**

Materials:

- ⚜ 1 roll brown craft paper
- ⚜ DecoArt Americana acrylic paint:
  - 1 bottle Berry Red
  - 1 bottle Bright Yellow
  - 1 bottle Lamp (Ebony) Black
- ⚜ Painter's Opaque Paint Markers, Medium:
  - 1 black
  - 1 red
  - 1 yellow
- ⚜ Wraphia:
  - 1 roll yellow
  - 1 roll red
  - 1 roll black

- ⚜ colored paper clips incorporating red, yellow and black
- ⚜ note card or card stock
- ⚜ 1 Scotch Pop-up Tape Strip Dispenser
- ⚜ water container
- ⚜ palette paper
- ⚜ paper towels

Tools:

- ⚜ Loew-Cornell medium sea sponge
- ⚜ Fiskars all-purpose scissors
- ⚜ Fiskars circle hand punch

Instructions:

① Measure and cut one piece of brown craft paper to fit the gift box. Place the paper flat on the work surface.

② Squeeze separate puddles of both the Berry Red and Bright Yellow acrylic paints onto a piece of palette paper.

③ Dampen the sponge with water, removing any excess on a paper towel.

④ Dip the sponge into the red paint. Using a swiping motion, apply swipes of red paint over the entire surface of the paper, leaving room for the yellow. Wash the sponge and remove any excess water on a paper towel.

⑤ Repeat the same step using yellow paint, filling in empty areas on the paper. Dip the same sponge back into the red paint. Continue applying color to the paper, this time mixing the yellow and red paint to create orange. Allow the paint to dry completely. Wash the sponge and blot it dry on a paper towel.

⑥ Using the black opaque paint marker, create squiggles and motifs over the painted and non-painted areas of the paper. Allow the marker to dry.

⑦ Wrap the gift. Refer to "Gift-Wrapping Basics: How to wrap a box."

⑧ Cut long-enough strands of each of the colored Wraphia to wrap around the box, criss-cross under the box, and tie a knot on top.

⑨ To make the bow, cut 10 12" lengths of black, yellow and red Wraphia. Group one strand of each color together. Feed the three strands under the knot at the top of the box. Tie the strands securely. Continue this process with the rest of the ribbon to create a spidery bow.

⑩ Attach paper clips to the Wraphia tails and bow.

PACKAGE #2

① Same technique – different look! Repeat the same process as above, using the black paint to create the swipes of color on the craft paper.

② Use the red and yellow paint markers to design funky motifs all over the wrap.

③ Create the bow in the same manner, perhaps adding different-colored paper clips.

GIFT TAG IDEA

The gift tag for these gifts can be just as funky and colorful as the wrapping paper. If you are wrapping a large parcel, create the gift tag of a size and nature that suits the package. Try using a standard-size note card.

1. Using the black, red and yellow markers, create motifs and squiggles on the face of the note card. Leave the inside blank to write your message.
2. Punch a hole in the upper left-hand corner of the card.
3. Feed a strand of each color of Wraphia through the hole, and tie a shoelace bow.
4. Attach several colored paper clips to the card, and slip the card in behind the bow.

WHITE TO **WONDERFUL**

Materials:

- ✢ gift boxes, sizes of your choice
- ✢ several sheets white photocopy paper
- ✢ Wraphia:
    - • 1 roll Light Green
    - • 1 roll Straw Yellow
    - • 1 roll Terra Cotta
- ✢ Rust-oleum Painter's Touch:
    - • 1 can Sun Yellow
    - • 1 can Burgundy
    - • 1 can Meadow Green

- ✢ comb-spring hairclips in coordinating colors
- ✢ 1 roll Scotch Long-Mask Masking Tape
- ✢ 1 Scotch Permanent Adhesive Glue Stick
- ✢ large trash bag
- ✢ disposable latex gloves

Tools:

- ✢ Fiskars all-purpose scissors
- ✢ Fiskars circle hand punch
- ✢ glue gun and glue sticks

Instructions:

① Work in a well-ventilated area, and choose a large flat surface to work on.

② Lay the first box as flat as possible. Shake the cans of spray paint well.

③ Wearing the latex gloves, spray an even coat of Meadow Green paint over the entire surface of the gift box. Ensure that all areas of the box are sprayed. If necessary, allow portions of the box to dry before doing the rest of the box. Allow the paint to dry.

④ Place a piece of photocopy paper flat on the work surface. Apply a light coat of the Sun Yellow spray paint to the entire surface of the paper. Allow the paint to dry thoroughly.

⑤ Create a criss-cross pattern, using the masking tape, by applying pieces of tape from one side of the paper across to the other, and from one end down to the bottom. This can be done in an even fashion, or randomly.

⑥ Spray a coat of the Meadow Green spray paint over the entire surface of the paper. Allow the paint to dry slightly, then gently remove the masking tape to reveal the yellow color underneath the tape.

⑦ Once the green paint is dry, repeat the same process with the masking tape, placing the strips of tape in a different pattern on the paper.

⑧ Spray a coat of the Burgundy paint over the entire surface of the paper. Allow the paint to dry slightly. Remove the masking tape to reveal the complete pattern.

⑨ Reassemble the gift box if required, and use the glue stick to adhere the patterned paper to the front and sides of the box.

⑩ Tie a piece of each color of Wraphia around the top and bottom edges of the paper.

GIFT TAG IDEA

1. Using a piece of card stock approximately 2" x 4", glue several pieces of colored Wraphia on to the card using the glue stick.
2. Glue some pieces lengthwise and some widthwise, to create an attractive pattern.
3. Leave the bottom left-hand corner open for your message.

PACKAGE #2 (green medium box)

① Spray paint a second gift box Meadow Green.

② Use the same technique to create a plaid pattern on a piece of photocopy paper.

③ Adhere the paper to the box as suggested in the instructions above.

④ To create the funky bow on this package, make two groups of many 4" loops using all three colors of Wraphia. Tie each group off around the bottom, and insert the groups into a comb-spring hairclip. Attach the bow to the package using a glue gun.

PACKAGE #3 (small box)

① If the gift you are wrapping is quite small, you can use a decorated piece of paper to wrap the entire gift.

② Make a smaller bow by cutting 40 5" pieces of assorted colored Wraphia.

③ Grasp the pieces together in the middle using a small comb-spring hairclip.

④ Attach the bow to the package using a glue gun.

www.suewarden.com

American Art Clay Co., Inc.
4717 West 16th St.
Indianapolis, IN 46222
Phone: (317) 244-6871
Fax: (317) 248-9300

Armour Products
P.O. Box 128
210 Rawlins Park
Wyckoff, NJ 07481
Phone: (201) 847-0404
www.armourproducts.com

BagWorks Inc.
Fort Worth, Texas USA
Phone (817) 446-8080 or
(800) 365-7423 in USA & Canada
Fax (817) 446-8105 or
(800) 678-7364 in USA & Canada
www.bagworks.com

Big Resources Inc.
Free Clip Art Source
www.fresherimage.com

DecoArt
P.O. Box 386
Stanford, KY 40484
Phone: (606) 365-3193
www.decoart.com

Delta Technical Coatings, Inc.
2550 Pallissier Place
Whittier, CA 90601-1505
Phone: (562) 695-7969
www.deltacrafts.com

The Dow Chemical Company
Styrofoam (insert trademark symbol)
Brand Products / Crafts
Direct Mail Services / McKay Press
215 State Street
Midland, MI 48641
www.styrofoamcrafts.com

Environmental Technology, Inc.
1646 Barrett Drive
North Saanich, BC V8L 5A6
Phone: (250) 655-3722
Email: canadamail@eti-usa.com
www.eti-usa.com

Environmental Technology, Inc.
South Bay Depot Road
Fields Landing, CA 95537
Phone: (707) 443-9323
Email: mail@eti-usa.com
www.eti-usa.com

Essential Packaging
#205 17665 66A Avenue
Surrey, BC V3S 2A7
Phone: Canada Wide (888) 288-2247
Greater Vancouver (604) 575-1117
www.essentialpackaging.com

Fiskars Canada Inc.
275 Renfrew Drive, Suite 208
Markham, ON L3R 0C8
Phone: (905) 940-8460
Fax: (905) 940-8469
www.fiskars.com

Fiskars Consumer Products Inc.
School, Office & Crafts Division
7811 West Stewart Avenue
Wausau, WI 54401
Phone: (715) 842-2091
www.fiskars.com

FPC Corporation
355 Hollow Hill Dr.
Wanconda, IL 60084
Phone: (847) 487-4583
Fax: (847) 487-0174
Email: glueguns@aol.com
Suppliers of glue guns and glue sticks
www.surebonder.com

Hot Off The Press
1259 NW Third,
Canby, OR 97013
Phone: (503) 266-9102 or
(800) 227-9595
Email: infor@hotp.com
www.CraftPizazz.com

Hunt Canada International
690 Gana Court
Mississauga, ON L5S 1P2
Phone: (905) 564-7717
Fax: (905) 564-7094
www.hunt-corp.com

Loew-Cornell
563 Chestnut Avenue
Teaneck, NJ 07666-2490
Phone: (201) 836-7070
www.loew-cornell.com

McCall Pattern Company
c/o 205 Bethridge Rd.
Etobicoke, ON M9W 1N4
Phone: (905) 666-3066
www.mccall.com

Offray Ribbon
Lion Ribbon Company, Inc.
C.M. Offray & Son Inc.
Route 24, Box 601
Chester, NJ 07930-0601
Phone: (908) 879-4700
www.offray.com

Jerry Payton, Creativity Inc.
EVP Business Development, Mergers &
Acquisitions
7855 Hayvenhurst Ave.
Van Nuys, CA 91406
Phone: (818) 778-3222
jerry.payton@westrimcrafts.com

Plaid Enterprises, Inc.
3225 Westech Drive
Norcross, GA 30092
Phone: (800) 842-4197
www.plaidonline.com

Provo Craft
295 W. Center Street
Provo, UT 84601
Phone: (801) 373-5908
www.provocraft.com

Regal Greetings and Gifts
7035 Ordan Drive
Mississauga, ON L5T 1T1
Regal product used on the following
pages: 20-27, 44-46, 54-55, 59-63, 76-79,
82-85, 88-95, 113-118, 122, 126-129,
136-141
Phone: (905) 670-1126
www.RegalGreetings.com

Rust-Olem Brands
Corporate Headquarters
11 Hawthorn Parkway
Vernon Hills, IL 60061
Phone: (847) 367-7700, or
(800) 553-8444
Fax: (847) 816-2330
www.rustoleum.com
www.paintideas.com

Panacea Products Corp.
2711 International Street
Columbus, OH 43228
Phone: (614) 850-7000

Sanford Corporation
2711 Washington Blvd.
Bellwood, IL 60104
A Division of Newell-Rubbermaid
Phone: (800) 323-0749
www.sanfordcorp.com

3M Canada Company
P.O. Box 5757
London, ON N6A 4T1
Customer Contact Centre: (800) 364-3577
www.mmm.com

Walnut Hollow®
1409 State Road 23
Dodgeville, WI 53533-2112
Phone: (608) 935-9064
www.walnuthollow.com

Winward, A Lifestyle Company
6225 Danville Road
Mississauga, ON L5T 2H7
Phone: (905) 670-0888
www.winwardsilks.com